WITH LOVE – and ELBOW GREASE

A Guide to Antiquing, Decorating,
and Finishing Almost Anything

by Elizabeth Lowry Browning

DRAWINGS BY
THE AUTHOR

PHOTOGRAPHS BY
ILEY BROWNING

SIMON AND SCHUSTER   NEW YORK

TO ILEY

CONTENTS

FOREWORD

Robert Browning (no kin!) has put into words far better than my halting prose my feeling about this or any other creative endeavor.

> *. . . we're made so that we love*
> *First when we see them painted, things we have passed*
> *Perhaps a hundred times nor cared to see;*
> *And so they are better, painted—better to us,*
> *Which is the same thing. Art was given for that—*
> *God uses us to help each other so,*
> *Lending our minds out. . . .*
>
> "Fra Lippo Lippi"

This book would not have been, without the affectionate support of my dear friend Betty Helm, who really started the ball rolling; Marilyn and Kurt Kluger, who urged and encouraged me to teach and write; Edwin Karges, Jr., of Karges Furniture, whose technical knowledge and advice has been in-

9

valuable; and, most important, my husband (who has lived through the mess!) and four children—Graeme, Trip, Lowry Ann, and Windy—who have performed services ranging from sanding drawers to reading proof. Windy, at age two, can only clasp her small hands and exclaim, "How pretty!" when she views an illustration—but this is enough to make me feel like Mary Cassatt!

E. L. B.
Evansville, Indiana
October 1967

WITH LOVE –
and
ELBOW GREASE

1

A BACCHANALIAN GARLAND

What is antiquing?

THE word *antiquing* is, in its own genre, as much a postwar addition to the language as *Sputnik* or *astronaut*—although it is not nearly so precise. It sprang, not from the Greek or Russian but, Minerva-like, from the brain of some unsung Madison Avenue adman in a flash of brilliance.

Antiquing, prewar, generally meant faking—a clever process practiced by crafty (and greedy) dealers, involving a ball peen hammer and a metal rasp—but this is no longer a valid definition. Obviously, no one in his right mind is going to *antique* anything that is truly an antique. Covering a beautiful piece of Baltimore Hepplewhite, or a Chapin highboy with a coat of paint would be sheer madness—if only from a monetary point of view. To my mind, painting over any beautiful wood—cherry, mahogany, even some walnut—is sinful. So *antiquing* is really an accepted euphemism, describing the process of painting and glazing a piece that would otherwise be shoved in the garage or the barn (nobody can afford attics any more)

13

until it fell apart of old age. It is *redoing*, or making something lovely and useful out of an object that is less than that—how much less depends on the piece.

This renovation is begun by first covering whatever-it-is with a coat of flat paint, decorating or not decorating the what's-it, and rubbing the paint with a colored glaze. After the glaze is applied, and wiped off to the desired finish, a final coat of satin varnish seals your work, protecting it from hammer blows, dirty heels, wet glasses, burning cigarettes, and other routine hazards. It is a simple process, and it's not hard to do, but it does require enthusiasm, love, and elbow grease. I've been doing this kind of thing, off and on, for ten years—and it has given me untold hours of pleasure. I've done Christmas presents, baby

presents, pieces for my own house, and pieces to sell—and they've all been different, and fun to do. I've whiled away a good many hours that would otherwise have been tedious, at best. While I was waiting for my last baby, for instance, I redid the old crib and a small, marble-top washstand for the little clothes. I happily painted the washstand blue, and put pink strawberries and roses on it—figuring this was an equitable compromise. Our small daughter's clothes are stowed away in it nicely, and my time was well spent.

I painted furniture long before the kits came on the market—although I think they're great. For you who are uninitiated, kits are now put out by several large and small paint companies. An antiquing kit supplies the purchaser with a can of flat base enamel, in a variety of colors, with a can of glaze that is color-keyed to blend with the base. Back in the old days, one had to search the paint stores for a usable color and finish as a base coat, and mix one's own glaze from scratch. This was time-consuming, and often maddening. Antiquing kits have filled this gap with a tantalizing variety of colors and glazes.

As I also paint—pictures—in watercolors and oils, as well as in flat enamel, I was inevitably drawn to decorating my furniture. My kitchen table and chairs, once monstrously knotty pine, were my first project. In the ensuing years, I've painted out the old and splashed on the new several times—and I'm getting ready to do them again. That's one great advantage to this game. When you're terribly tired of something, or you've picked a color that's impossible for you to live with any longer, or Aunt Hattie has given you a gift you cannot refuse—a transformation can be wrought with very little cash outlay.

As I like bright colors, and lots of decoration, I found my métier in folk art. Although many people think of the Pennsylvania Dutch as the sole originators and propagators of the faith, this is only one small section of an art that is worldwide. Called *folk art* because its practitioners were, largely, untutored by academic art standards, it sprang—independently and spontaneously— from a desire for beauty among the peoples of Russia, Hungary, Sweden, all of Western Europe, England, and the

American colonies. Our early settlers brought with them designs that are found in Europe from the Middle Ages on—hearts, grapes, wheat, and others. They reproduced motifs that were intertwined with all they had loved and left behind. There is a famous Massachusetts chest—the Taunton chest—now in the Metropolitan Museum of Art, with an intricate decoration on the front that is, to me, a dead ringer for Jacobean crewel. The cabinetmaker Robert Crosman produced several of these chests, dating from about 1725 to 1740. This work, done on harsh New England soil, must have helped to soften the bleakness of that hostile environment.

Sometimes highly sophisticated, sometimes crude, this varied decorative art got to me. Before I knew what I was about, I had garlanded the house with hearts and flowers—while my husband groaned. I have since branched out into scrolls, fruit, shells, horses, *millefleurs*, and a variety of other motifs—but my wayward heart, I fear, lies in a Bacchanalian garland of roses, grapes, and ivy.

From this foliate madness to teaching was a brief step. Many of my friends—particularly those who have all their children in school, and extra time available—have become carried away with painting furniture. I decorated a buffet for one friend, she asked me if I would consider teaching a workshop class, and I was, suddenly, catapulted into business.

Since my unexpected foray as an educator began, I've taught mainly beginners—and they have turned out some lovely things. At first, because I had painted for so long that I took many things for granted, I neglected to teach some things beginners want most to know. (This is, I think, probably a fault with most experienced painters. I have had to force myself to verbalize what is an unconscious process.) I didn't *know* how I mixed colors—I simply mixed, knowing the result would be right, with no conscious thought. Now I can tell others how to mix color, shade, and accomplish their other aims in specific terms. I've learned so much from working with my classes—and I hope to pass this on.

Almost anything can be antiqued. You may start with

what I call a "country piece"—a chair, or a pie safe, or a little washstand—that has good lines but has been made by some semiskilled craftsman out of poplar, or gum, or another readily available wood that has no particular intrinsic beauty. The piece may be marred or chipped, or have a few cracks, nail holes, or other defects—may even be missing a leg! You could begin with a gingerbready Victorian chair, or a contemporary dresser that has outlived its limed-oak finish. Whatever, the basic lines must be interesting—here lies the first essential. If the basic lines are good—clean and simple, or with lovely curves that may have been covered by black varnish or tacked-on carving—something charming can be made from the piece. If the lines are ugly, quit before you start!

You'll never be pleased, as there is no paint in the world that

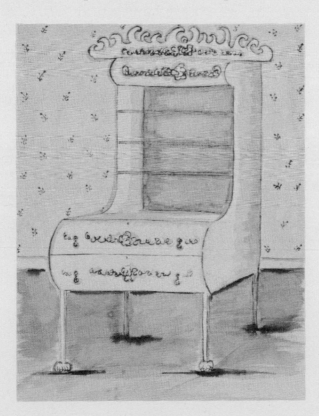

Forget it!

can cover awkward, ungainly proportion. Color can cheat a little, but never enough to balance a topheavy secretary or conceal a ponderous leg. Learn to develop a sharp eye for good design, and forget the trimmings.

With this firmly in mind, choose a piece for painting. All antiquing enthusiasts, misnomer though *antiquing* may be —and all who are anxious to dive into the paint bucket—forward! Let us cast off the garlands of ivy and roses, and get to the elbow grease.

Paint it!

2

TO STRIP
OR NOT TO STRIP?

Preparing and painting wood surfaces

Whenever there are any minor painting jobs to be done around our house—porch furniture, screen doors— my husband (who cleverly claims he does these things badly because he's left-handed) says, "So you paint so well—this needs painting!" Naturally, I can't possibly know what you—gentle reader—have done before. Some of you are, I'm sure, experienced. Others of you have never even painted a screen door. Those of you who are old hands can now turn the page, because I'm going to start at the very beginning. (You new hands, do not feel overwhelmed. On page 26, at the end of this chapter, and following other chapters, you'll find a specific checklist, not only of materials but of step-by-step procedure.)

When I start on a piece of furniture, I have two serious faults—I'm lazy, and I'm impatient. I knit socks, because it takes all the willpower I have to finish a sweater. I do needle-point purses, but my piano bench is literally threadbare, because I haven't worked myself up to tackling such a broad expanse of needlepoint. Therefore, because of my character defects—and because this approach is just as satisfactory, if not sometimes superior—I do not strip off the old finish, unless it's simply impossible. I hate to strip off old paint. It's a dirty, smelly, boring procedure, and I'm against it.

This is my system. First, remove all hardware, and any doors—and leave them off until the job is completed. Any deep nail holes or cracks should be filled now, and the best bet for any patching is plastic wood. Putty shrinks as it dries, and is likely to leave a hairline crack all around the patched spot, making things almost worse than they were. Fill the bad places, leaving the plastic wood raised slightly above the surface. Use a putty knife, palette knife, or your fingers. When the plastic wood is completely dry, it can be sanded down level with the surface and, when painted, is invisible.

Now, instead of stripping off the old finish, I take the roughest sandpaper I can find (extra-coarse garnet paper is best) and sand off all the bumps, nicks, and splintery edges—until I can rub my hand over the surface and it feels satiny. This is a tactile judgment. Never mind how it looks—it's all in how it feels! Remember, too, rounded edges and worn spots not only pick up glaze beautifully, but make the finished product look older—and this is very desirable. I am told, in strict confidence, that some antique dealers (again, those endowed with natural guile!) take their finds and file off the edges with a steel rasp, to increase the ante. This is called *chamfering*, and a

Sandpaper block

chamfered edge is one that's worn down by years of loving use. So—I sand away, chamfering at the bit as I work. (Forgive me.) I do not own an electric sander, but I find that sandpaper, wrapped around a small block of wood, is very efficient and saves hands.

After I've finished sanding, and all the rough spots are gone, I wash the whole thing down, inside and out, with mineral spirits. If it's really filthy, and has been sitting in somebody's chicken house—or worse—for several years, I scrub it with a brush and one of the disinfectant detergents available, bottled, in every supermarket. If water is involved in the cleaning, your piece must dry for a day or two before you can start painting—but it's worth it. The little washstand I did for the baby had obviously been in the chicken house—there were feathers wedged in the back and, to my horror, what seemed to be rat holes! When I saw this, I ran for the hose, and used my detergent full strength.

I mentioned *mineral spirits* a minute ago, and this is as good a place as any to sing its praises. Also called Oleum, or paint thinner, this marvelous product sells for about $1.00 or $1.25 a gallon in any paint or hardware store. (Here, in the Middle West, if you take your gallon jug to the local paint supplier, he will fill it with mineral spirits for 28 cents a gallon!) It not only cleans brushes, thins paint, and does anything turpentine will do, but it will remove chewing gum from clothes, clean up old pieces of furniture, remove wax, and is a generally handy product. Also—obviously—it is a good deal cheaper than turpentine. If you get paint on your clothes, or the rug, or—as we did—a brand-new red corduroy bedspread, soak the spot in mineral spirits and out the paint comes. I buy it by the gallon —it is flammable (but not explosive as gasoline) and I wouldn't let the children drink it—but I couldn't live without it.

After you've sanded well, and cleaned the surface, then get your base paint or primer, your rubber gloves, coarse steel wool or an old rag, and liquid sander. This is the only time I use rubber gloves, as they annoy me, but liquid sander will leave your hands like raw meat if you fool with it long enough.

All this equipment has to be assembled before you start because, once you get going, you have to keep going. Liquid sander (sold under different brand names by paint companies) applied with coarse steel wool or a rough rag, penetrates the old finish, softens it, and leaves it tacky—although it does not necessarily remove it. While the old finish is tacky and soft, you paint into this wet area and the paint will adhere perfectly—better, in some cases, than it will on a fresh, unpainted surface. The only catch to all this is that the repainting has to be done within 15 to 30 minutes after the liquid sander has been applied—or the whole effect dissolves like an ephemeral vision, and the old finish hardens again. I do a section at a time—say, scrub down the top with liquid sander, and paint. Then a side, and paint. This is a base coat, anyhow, and doesn't need to be perfect. If I'm going to use liquid sander, I rather like to use a prime coat— although the companies that make antiquing kits insist this is unnecessary, and who am I to defy them for you! Suit yourself. On most of my pieces I use a primer—on a few I don't. I'll have to leave this choice to your discretion—and energy.

A *primer* is a preparatory coat of shellac, or other sealer—I am vague because the chemistry of paint is now so varied—applied *first* to the surface that will be, then, painted. It is usually white, or a neutral gray—Tinner's Red being the exception— and it dries flat, leaving a smooth surface. As a prime coat seals, and plain paint does not, I use a primer. The application takes very little time, and I think you get a better, more professional paint job.

Tinner's Red is an excellent primer for any metal, or wood. Because it is a dark, red-oxide color, it is best used under a dark paint. (See page 30.) Under a light paint, a white or gray primer is preferable. Plain shellac will do on unpainted, unfinished wood, or over old paint. The addition of pigment and other ingredients make a prepared primer easier to use and *see* for the novice.

If you reject a primer, you may have to use 3 coats of paint to cover—but even if you use a primer, you must have 2 coats of paint in addition. Apply a first and a second coat—see Check-list on p. 27. Don't skip a step!

I use a primer that is a pigmented shellac. It seals any un-desirable stains or marks, as well as priming, and is the best I've ever found. It is in an alcohol base (as is all shellac) and can be painted over in 45 minutes—so the additional trouble is hardly worth complaining about. The only drawback to such a primer is the alcohol base—mineral spirits will not clean your brushes. You must wash them in ammonia and water, or wood alcohol—a thing that's banned from our house.

My husband, a geochemist, has an obsession about wood alcohol, and I believe it is justified. He will not allow a can in our house, despite my original pleading that I couldn't work without it. Wood alcohol is a *deadly poison*—even the fumes can blind. He contends that it is entirely too dangerous to be in any home with children. If a child—or animal—does drink it, there are no telltale fumes to give this fact away. Wood alcohol is not unpalatable, as kerosene, Lysol, or other poisons are, and the symptoms are usually delayed—becoming evident when it's too late to avoid the horrible consequences. I have found that ammonia works fine in cleaning varnish and primer brushes. If it doesn't, I'd rather throw the brush away than take this risk. However, you'll find all sorts of advice about using wood alco-hol in any book on furniture refinishing, and any drugstore sells it by the quart. All commercial paint removers contain methyl, or wood, alcohol, and that's why you're cautioned to use them in a "well-ventilated room." I won't have it, I don't recommend it, and I won't use it—if you do, please be careful. Anything with the word *methyl* contains wood alcohol—*do* read the instructions in small print on the back of the can!

New wood, as in unfinished furniture, should—as I've said —be given a sealer coat of shellac, instead of a primer, before the first coat of base paint is applied.

Use, for your base coat, a paint specifically mixed for an-tiquing—*no* latex, and *no* semigloss, please. (There are antiqu-ing kits out with a latex base paint, but I don't recommend them.) I have used, with great success, an oil-base *flat wall* paint. I think, for a first project, that you may be a little more confident with an antiquing paint and color-keyed glaze, but if you can't get it, oil-base wall paint—*flat*—will fill the bill.

I have found, too, that a color choice is not as simple as it might seem. If you can't visualize the finished product—and many people cannot—I would suggest that you choose a neutral color rather than a bright one. White, green, butter yellow, gray are all pretty safe. Save the more intense shades for later, when you can imagine the effect after the glaze is rubbed on the paint.

I buy medium-priced brushes. If they're too cheap, they are stiff (like a whisk broom), and spatter paint. If you ruin the most expensive brush you can buy, guilt assails. Medium-priced brushes can be thrown away without severe guilt pangs! See Checklist on page 26 for sizes.

As soon as your primer is dry, plunge in with the first coat. I cannot tell you how to paint—I don't suppose anyone can. It's a matter of practice. I can give you a few hints, gained more from watching beginners' mistakes than from any other source. Start from the bottom of the piece and work up.

Then, if you have any drips, they run into an already wet surface, and are much easier to smooth away. Tip your brush off on the edge of the can and smoothly brush—do not *dab*—the paint on the surface you are painting. Cover this surface well, and then smooth it out with the tip of the brush—do not try to make each stroke perfection. Use a clean or a new brush always. Be sure your paint is thin enough. If it's too thick, it'll drag, your brush marks will show, and you'll be frantic. Two or three tablespoons of mineral spirits will correct thick paint—and should be added, automatically, if you are not using a freshly opened can.

Don't worry if the first coat is imperfect—or the second, for that matter. There is no such thing as an absolutely perfect coat of paint, unless it's done by machine—and that mirror finish is usually spray lacquer, and not paint at all. Remember,

Start from the bottom and work up

when you're through with your work, be it a tray or a wardrobe, you will have completed a very personal piece of hand-
craft—as much as if you had woven a rug, or made a vase—and
no hand-done work is perfect. That's the point—you don't want
your piece to look as if it were done by a machine, and you're not
trying to create a slick, mass-produced product. I look for, and
encourage, imperfections. In the first place, they pick up the
glaze attractively and make a more interesting finish. In the
second place, they add to the look of age and they increase, to
me, the beauty of the hand work that has been done. I do sand

between coats, with a very fine garnet paper (6/o), because it facilitates a better paint job. Any unnoticed drips can be rubbed out by sanding, and, again, your eventual goal is a satiny-smooth, glowing finish—not a slick, hard, shiny surface.

After sanding with sandpaper, wipe your surface clean with a tack rag. These rags, sold in hardware or paint stores for about 30 cents, are simply wads of cheesecloth dipped in varnish and wrung dry. As they have a slightly sticky quality, they pick up any minute particles from a freshly sanded surface—better than blowing!

In between coats, and when you are finished, clean your brushes first with mineral spirits, then with hot water and a household cleaner containing naphtha. Rinse and, finally, stand them in a jar or can, handles down, to dry. Brushes will last for a good while with this simple care.

It is much easier—in fact, almost essential—to decorate on a flat, matte finish. The paint tends to slide and run on anything slicker. So—if you plan to decorate your work, stop now, after the second coat of paint.

Basic Materials Checklist

2 1" bristle brushes
2 2" bristle brushes
Sandpaper—coarse and fine (finishing) paper
Steel wool—coarse and fine
1 pint white or gray primer } All primers. Choice depends
1 pint Tinner's Red } on the surface you intend
or } to seal.
1 pint clear shellac }
1 pint can antiquing undercoat paint
1 half-pint can glaze } For finishing.
1 pint can satin varnish }
1 tack rag
old rags and paper towels

old newspapers
mineral spirits or turpentine
household ammonia
detergent containing naphtha
paint stirrers (tongue depressors are fine!)
empty tin cans (for cleaning brushes)

BASIC STEPS IN PREPARING AND PAINTING WOOD

1. Remove all hardware and doors.
2. Sand old finish with very coarse sandpaper until satin-smooth.
3. Soften old finish with a liquid sander, using a cloth or steel wool.
4. On new wood, as unfinished furniture, use a sealer coat of clear shellac; sand lightly with fine sandpaper.
5. Optional, old finish. Give one coat of primer; sand lightly with fine sandpaper.
6. Apply one coat of antiquing undercoat.
7. Sand lightly with fine sandpaper.
8. Apply second coat of base color.
9. Sand lightly with fine sandpaper.
10. Now you are ready to decorate!

3

THE BARE BONES

Preparing and painting metal surfaces

I F you're doing anything metal, unless it is brand-new, you must strip it—oh, agony! This is an absolute must because of rust—and all old metal has some rust spots somewhere. If you don't strip, the rust will eat through your new finish in time, and you're doomed—all that work for nothing.

For a small job, like a tray or metal box, any good commercial paint remover is probably the easiest thing to use. Although slower than lye, they are efficient, and can be used indoors. For a big job (and this works as well on wood as on metal) lye is the quickest paint remover. Lye's main drawback is its heat requirements—it will not work efficiently unless the temperature is 70 degrees or above. As I do not have a warm basement (or any basement, for that matter), I can use lye only in the summer. I put the piece to be stripped out in the gravel driveway, where I don't ever want grass, with the hose nearby. Mix 3 cans of lye with 3 quarts of water in a plastic pail, and add 1 cup wheat wallpaper paste, to insure a sticking consistency. (Without paste the lye-and-water mixture is too thin to adhere to the perpendicular sides of a chest or to table legs and other appendages.) Make a mop out of old rags and a stick, mop the caustic mixture on the old paint, let it set for a few minutes, and hose it off. (If you have no access to a hose, or are an apartment dweller, I would dismiss the lye method entirely and stick to a commercial product. Lye is too powerful to be used indoors, and plenty of water, *handy*, is a *must*.) Scrape off any remaining spots.

When all the old paint is removed, rinse your project with vinegar, to neutralize the remaining alkali. Keep a bucket of water close at hand, in case any lye splashes on you, and discourage participation by the baby—and your old, gummy paint comes off with ease.

If you have an old varnish finish (admittedly rare on metal, but we *are* talking about removing finishes!), ordinary household ammonia, poured into an enamel pan and daubed on with a dishmop, is the best remover I know of. The old black varnish melts right off. This, again, is an outdoor project—the fumes are too much. I save up my removing for summer—do it while I have the good weather—and then paint, at my leisure, in the gray of winter.

Back to rust. After all the paint has been removed—by the method of your choice—you must treat the metal to stop the rust action. Rust removers vary in availability according to the section of the country. Reference books written by New Yorkers, or New Englanders, specify a rust remover that hasn't ever been heard of in the Middle West. Here, such products are sold by the drum to oil producers and other industries, and are not available to the small retail trade. The one we can buy is called Metal Treat, and it is also excellent for preparing new galvanized ware for a prime coat. This product, in full strength, stops rust on old metal and, diluted, serves as a wash to prepare any metal for paint. I always prime metal—new or old—as the final coats seem to bond better to a primer.

If you are confronted, as I was, with a solidly rusted big area on an old metal trunk—forget it. You aren't going to remove the rust. The best remedy here is to use a product called Penetrol. This, painted on with a brush and left 24 hours to dry, not only stops the rust action but bonds it to the metal. After the Penetrol has dried, you may safely paint over the area, without fear of reprisal from rust.

A wonderful primer for metal (and wood) is called Tinner's Red. Most paint companies carry this, or an equivalent, under various brand names. It is the color of iron oxide—a beautiful dull red—and is not only a primer, but a rust preventative as well. It's also a great color for a dark or black finish—requiring fewer coats to cover than a white primer.

After your metal piece—new or old—is cleaned, treated for rust, and primed, the painting sequence is the same as it is on wood. One coat may suffice, but two coats are better—again, sand lightly between coats.

Stop after the second coat, as before. Now you are ready to decorate. On to the garlands and scrolls!

Basic Steps in Preparing and Painting Metal

1. Strip off all old paint with paint stripper.
2. Treat for rust. On small spots, use Metal Treat. On large areas, where the rust has bonded to the metal, paint on Penetrol with a brush, and let dry for 12 hours.
3. On any new metal—galvanized tubs, etc.—wash well with one part Metal Treat to seven parts water. Let dry.
4. Prime with either a white primer or Tinner's Red. Tinner's Red is excellent over rust—but be sure to stir it completely, getting all the lumps out of the bottom.
5. Sand lightly with fine sandpaper—finishing paper.
6. Apply first coat of antiquing undercoat.
7. Sand lightly with finishing paper. Catch all drips now.
8. Apply second coat of base color.

9. Sand lightly with finishing paper.
10. You are now ready to decorate!

STIR ALL PAINT!

4
WHAT IS PINK?
A ROSE IS PINK

Color, and how it works—
paints, brushes, and techniques

What is pink?   a rose is pink,
By a fountain's brink.
CHRISTINA G. ROSSETTI

H AD I been asked by my Maker—or had I been able to choose—I would have begged to be born with great, natural athletic ability, and legs like Marlene Dietrich's. This is, I suppose, the curse of the human condition; each of us longs for that which he does not have. The Lord blessed me, instead, with the kind of coordination that makes it hard for me to catch a ball, legs that carry me but do not satisfy me aesthetically, and an inborn, intuitive eye for color. This eye—this

32

instinctive ability to see and reproduce the spectrum—like perfect pitch, or beautiful bone structure, is God-given. It cannot, unfortunately, be taught.

However—and I cannot emphasize this too much—we are all born with a certain amount of ability for all things. I have taken the coordination (such as it is) that I was given and can swim, ride a horse, and play a game of tennis that doesn't absolutely send me off the court in tears—but I've worked at it! Because I desperately wanted to do these things, I've put in the extra time and concentration that are required for *me*, against that instinctive knack of making their muscles react exactly as they dictate that is God-given to some of my peers. The same thing works in mixing, seeing, and using color. If you will open your eyes, try to see a little differently, and develop the color sense that we all have to a degree—unless we are color-blind— the world of color will no longer be the baffling and alarming problem that it seems to most neophytes.

Since you're doing furniture, or what have you, and not painting the Sistine Chapel, I don't feel that you need to know any more than color basics in order to be able to mix the shades you're likely to be using. There are, for the aspiring and professional artist, whole books on color alone. If you get that carried away—and I hope you will—head for the local library. I'm not going to confuse you! My only aim is to give you a foundation upon which to build.

In European folk art, in the decorations of Colonial America, even in the more sophisticated pieces from France, very simple, straightforward, almost raw colors were used consistently—there is very little subtlety, or shading. These artists employed materials at hand for pigments (the coloring substances, usually in powder form, that are mixed or ground with the liquids—usually linseed oil—called vehicles, to form paint). The reds and yellows were either metallic (iron oxide) or earth (yellow clay) colors. Greens were either mixed or made from metals. Blue was rarely used in this country, as the only reliable pigment was indigo. Then, indigo had to be brought round the Horn from India on a sailing vessel—and these craftsmen were not often able to get their hands on it, or couldn't pay for the precious dye when it was to be had.

Therefore, I start my students with this very simple palette:

cadmium red
yellow ochre (also called yellow oxide)
cadmium yellow
cobalt blue
chrome green
burnt umber
titanium white
Mars black

These are the standard names used in fine arts terminology to distinguish one shade of color from another. (We will discuss later the forms in which they can be bought.) They are all true, clear pigments. Many other colors change when they are mixed, or have overtones that become pronounced, or bleed into and through a covering layer and are difficult for the inexperienced. With the above palette, you can mix almost any shade you need—the exception is a brilliant violet, which is seldom used —and you won't have the paint going muddy or gray while you're mixing. Velasquez used only three colors—and black and white—to paint his masterpieces, so you should be able to do at least as well with this wide range!

This palette is excellent for building a color wheel—and this you *must* know. The only magic about mixing color happens in the color wheel, and if you memorize this, you can mix with abandon.

There are three primary colors—called *primary* because we don't know any way to combine two other colors and make any of these three.

PRIMARY COLORS

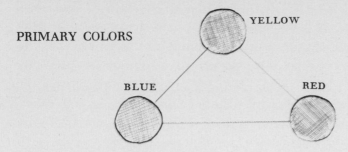

From these three, we can make three other colors, called —naturally—*secondary* colors.

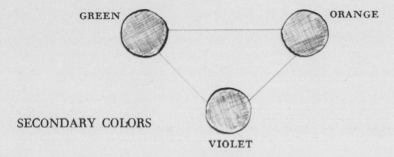

SECONDARY COLORS

Combine the two triangles, and you have:

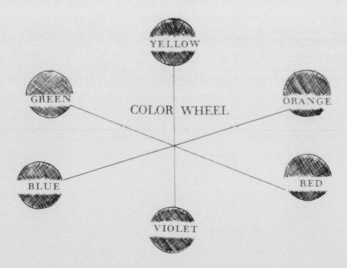

This is the color wheel—simple!

The color wheel is arranged logically, as you can see, with colors made from primary colors placed between the primaries that are their stems. (You all learned this in second grade—remember?—so consider this only review.) So, opposite colors on the color wheel are called *complements*. The meaning of the term is intrinsic in the word—these colors complete each other. They also (a happy play on words) compliment, or flatter, each other. They will also intensify and completely neutralize each other. Thus, green and red are complementary colors; so are yellow and violet (or purple), and blue and orange. If you mix complementary colors in equal amounts—one-half green, one-half red—you get mud, literally. The result is an ugly brown and—oddly enough—it is the same shade of brown no matter which two complements you mix. However, if you want to dull or mute a color, you can mix in a little of its complement, and the result is wonderful.

Conversely, if you wish to bring out a color or make it more prominent, put it beside its complement. It will be twice as vivid.

This is as much as I teach my classes about color. (Artists may collapse in horror! Ignore them!) I have found, if you learn these simple facts, and experiment with them, you can handle any color-mixing you need for decorating. To help my students in combining dull and paler shades for their designs, I've made up simple formulas for mixing colors. You will, of course, have to try these out on a pad of newsprint—this is a whole class session when I'm teaching. As you work, you'll see that the colors interact in a marvelous way, and the whole spectrum is at your fingertips once you're familiar with your paints.

To Mix a Muted or Dull Shade:

Green: Begin with chrome green. Add a touch or two of cadmium red. Then add burnt umber until desired shade is reached.

Red: Begin with cadmium red. Add a touch or two of chrome green. Then add burnt umber, a touch at a time, until the desired shade is reached. A touch of cadmium yellow will bring out the orange tones.

Yellow: Begin with yellow ochre (or yellow oxide). Add burnt umber, a touch at a time, until you have the shade you want. A touch of chrome green, or cobalt blue—depending on the other colors in the design—may be helpful here.

Blue: Begin with cobalt blue. Add a little white. Then add burnt umber, and a touch of chrome green, until the desired tone is achieved.

Purple: Begin with cadmium red. Add white to make a deep pink. Then add cobalt blue, a touch at a time, until you have the shade you need. A touch of chrome green may turn the trick.

Orange: Begin with cadmium yellow, and add a little white. Then add cadmium red, a touch at a time, until you have the desired shade. A touch of chrome green will dull it at once.

A touch of color

To Lighten Colors:

Green: To chrome green, add cadmium yellow. Then add white, if a paler shade is needed.

Red: To cadmium red, add cadmium yellow or yellow ochre—depending on background and adjacent colors. For pink, add white.

Blue: To cobalt blue, add white only.

Yellow: To cadmium yellow, add white. To yellow ochre, also add white, until desired shade is reached.

Violet: Begin with cadmium red. Add enough white to make a pale pink. Then add cobalt blue, a touch at a time, until you have a pale mauve or violet.

Orange: Begin with cadmium yellow, and add enough white to make a very pale yellow. Then add cadmium red, a bare touch, to make a very pale apricot.

Black and white are non-colors. White contains every color in the spectrum, and black is the absence of color. I include black for accents, and to be used as black—not to mix to darken any shade. Black will turn your color sooty—if you don't choose to use a complement, use burnt umber. This is a warm brown, and mixes well with anything. Burnt umber with white makes a warm gray; black with white makes a cold, steel gray.

Before you tackle any decorating, practice with these formulas on a big pad of newsprint, available in any art supply or discount store—sometimes, even drugstores. Then you won't be disappointed, or in doubt, when the moment of truth arrives.

Which brings us to paints—as you would find it hard to mix color without them! I use, have used for years, and teach my students to use, artist's acrylic paints in tubes or jars. These are the newest thing—postwar—on the artist's horizon. They are made in the same color range as oils, have the consistency of oils, and look like oil when they're dry. Unlike oil, they are water-soluble, dry in about ten or fifteen minutes, and can be removed—*while still wet*—with a damp rag if you make a mistake. I underline the *still wet* bit because, once these paints are dry, they are as permanent as oils! I think they're ideal for the beginner, and eminently suited for decorating. There are several brands available—Liquitex, Shiva Acrylics, New Masters, Weber, Hyplar, Aquatec—and one company also produces them in jars. The jar paint has the consistency of tempera, or poster paint, especially good for this kind of work, as you want a flowing, loose stroke when you decorate. Whatever brand you buy, ask your art supply store for acrylics—they'll know what you're talking about.

Any paint requires a *medium*—or something to mix with it. Water thins watercolor; turpentine thins oil; casein medium, or water, thins casein; and an *acrylic matte varnish* or *polymer medium* thins acrylics. In effect, this medium does not thin, but extends the paint from the tube or jar, giving it a flowing consistency and making it easier to use. When you buy your basic colors, also purchase a bottle or jar of polymer medium or, preferably, matte varnish to use with your paints.

If, by any chance, some of you prefer to use artist's oils, sold in tubes—fine. I suggest, however, that you use damar varnish with japan drier with them.

Damar (also spelled dammar) varnish, sold in art supply stores, is a solution of damar resin in turpentine. Damar is a resin gathered from tropical forests, produced by trees of the genera *Shorea*, *Balanocarpus* and *Hopea*. It comes only from Malaya, Borneo, Java, and Sumatra, and is sold in pale, straw-colored lumps. Dissolved in turpentine, damar makes a very pure, colorless varnish that is used with quality artist's oils. Several good companies make the varnish, already prepared and bottled, for sale to artists and others. Damar has been used by artists since the Renaissance, under such names as "Damas" or "Gum de Mar."

Japan drier—a boiled solution of resins and shellac, not from Japan at all—is also sold in art supply houses to be used with artist's oils, and is a siccative agent that speeds the paint's drying time. It is particularly useful when you are painting in reds and certain blacks that are normally very slow-drying pigments.

Both damar varnish and japan drier should be mixed with tube oils as the medium while you are painting.

For those who have never held brush in hand, take heart —it's not as terrifying as you think. I have a few suggestions that have helped my absolute rank beginners in the past. Many new hands want to squeeze the paint from the tube onto a plate and use it—raw, just as it is—because they're afraid to mix. *Don't* do this all the time—you won't be happy. Always use a palette—a TV-dinner pan, an old white plate, pie tin, glossy magazine, or whatever suits you.

Squeeze or pour out a small amount of *each* color on the palette.

Arrange your colors in a logical order each time. For instance:

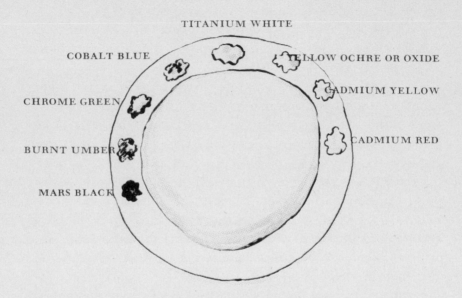

The above arrangement places the cool colors on one side of white, and the warm colors on the other. You may arrange your colors in any way that makes sense to you—but do it the same way each time. Then you'll always know where each color is, without searching for it, and your work will go faster.

To mix acrylic paints, wet your brush with water, then with matte varnish. Then, pull out some color onto your palette from the blob on the side. *Mix on the palette*, using matte varnish or polymer medium to thin your paint. *Always* mix shades on your palette. If you need a large amount of the same color, you may use a small container—but you'll know, then, how to mix the exact shade you need. Dip your brush into the blobs of paint on the palette, using a touch at a time.

Although you may use colors just as they come from the tube, your work will gain in subtlety, and become much more personal if you will alter and mix your colors. BE BOLD! The worst that can happen is an ugly patch of color on your palette that you will not use. Many painting teachers don't allow beginners anything except a brush one-inch wide or bigger for the first year—to keep them from being afraid of the paint. I've even painted with two- and three-inch brushes on canvas and loved it. Don't be inhibited—loosen up!

Keep dipping your brush into the matte varnish or polymer medium as you paint—mixing constantly with the color on your palette. Clean your brush thoroughly before switching to another color. Wash it well with water, wipe it on an old rag, and remove any residue of the previous pigment.

Water—you can't paint with acrylics without it—is cheap, plentiful, and handy. Keep it clean. Muddy water will kill a color as quickly as a complement. Keep your water in a tin can —not a jar.

Then, if you tip or knock your water off, you don't have a double mess to clean up. (I picked this up while sketching outdoors in watercolor, and have never gone back to the familiar glass jar!) Save a sixteen-ounce juice can—or another of ample proportions—and change your water often.

If your paint is too thick, add a touch of water, rather than matte varnish or polymer medium. After you've fooled around with the paints for a while, you'll get the feel of the balance to be kept between water and varnish. Too much water makes your paint thin—actually watercolor. Too little water, or medium, will give an impasto effect (like cake frosting), which you don't want in decorating designs.

When you make a mistake, a damp cloth will wipe it off
—but he who hesitates is lost! Once, while decorating some
cabinet doors for a friend, I goofed and didn't decide to change
it until my paint was dry. I had to sand it off!

Naturally, you can't paint, or mix, or practice anything,
without brushes. (You *can*—some artists paint with sponges,
old rags, waxed paper, combs, and other interesting articles—
but we won't.) I start everyone out with three basic brushes:

> 1 #3 Sabeline watercolor brush
> 1 #8 Sabeline watercolor brush
> 1 ¾-inch flat ox-hair rigger (watercolor) brush

This gives you a small brush for fine lines, a medium brush for
leaves, flowers, swirls, and a flat brush for bolder effects.

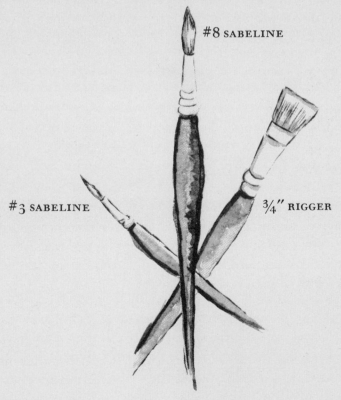

#8 SABELINE

#3 SABELINE

¾″ RIGGER

I do almost everything with the #8 and the rigger—but I find my students panic without a tiny brush. You may, as time goes on, want to experiment with other brushes, but these three will do anything you have in mind. If you feel you want to invest in only one brush, get the #8—it's very versatile.

Don't let anybody sell you a stiff-bristle oil brush—and *don't*, for Heaven's sake, use Johnny's old brushes that he had in the sixth grade when they made him take art and you had to buy him supplies. You won't be able to do one thing with them, and you'll give the whole project up in disgust! In this day in time, you seldom get what you pay for—artist's brushes are the rare exception. A cheap brush will shed bristles, leave a ragged edge instead of a clean line, and never hold a point. Oil brushes are wrong because they're too stiff. They are designed to manipulate thick oils, and your paint, ideally, will be more like heavy cream. On the other side of the coin, you don't need pure red sable brushes—they're divine, but terribly expensive. There is a #12 red sable brush that my mouth has been watering for—but it's $32.00, and I haven't yet been able to bring myself to part with that much for one brush. For your purposes, Sabeline will serve you well—for about half the price of red sable. (I use only Sabeline with my acrylics—my two red sables are too dear to me to dip into anything but water-color. Almost all red sable comes from Russia, and this has driven the price even higher.) Be sure to wash your brushes with a mild soap and water after use. Rinse them, bring them to a point or a chisel edge with your fingers, and stand them, handles down, in a tin can to dry.

One last bit of advice—a motto I have been thinking of having emblazoned on my forehead, along with STIR ALL PAINT!, each time I teach—PRACTICE MAKES PERFECT! The first time you try to mix color, you may get all mud. Don't worry. Most people do the same. Just wash your brush out (in clean water), throw away the paper, and start again. It will come—just as my tennis game has—if you really try.

COLOR

What is pink? a rose is pink
By a fountain's brink.
What is red? a poppy's red
In its barley bed.
What is blue? the sky is blue
Where the clouds float thro'.
What is white? a swan is white
Sailing in the light.
What is yellow? pears are yellow,
Rich and ripe and mellow.
What is green? the grass is green,
With small flowers between.
What is violet? clouds are violet
In the summer twilight.
What is orange? Why, an orange,
Just an orange!

CHRISTINA G. ROSSETTI

CHECKLIST OF PAINTS AND BRUSHES

Tube or jar acrylic paints, (2 fluid-ounce size)
including:

titanium white
Mars black
burnt umber
cadmium yellow

chrome green
cobalt blue
yellow oxide or ochre
cadmium red

1 8-ounce bottle matte varnish or polymer medium
1 #3 Sabeline watercolor brush
1 #8 Sabeline watercolor brush
1 ¾" flat Sabeline or camel-hair rigger brush—
optional
1 #1 Sabeline watercolor brush—optional

1 #00 striping brush—optional
1 #1 striping brush—optional

5

A LOAF OF BREAD
AND HYACINTHS

Designs and motifs—
transferring, placing, extending, adapting

Dᴇsɪɢɴs and design sources are as myriad as the leaves on a tree, a rosebud, cobwebs against a shifting light—or a shell brought home tucked in the corner of a suitcase from some happy beach, and placed where it recalls the sound of the sea in the depth of winter. I have around me, in the cubbyhole where I work, three such shells, a tiny blue delft vase, a Navajo Indian rug, my mother's Chinese porcelain god of wisdom, bedecked in a multicolored, flowered robe, a Japanese paper wastebasket covered with a repeat print, a Norwegian tin box, wreathed with rosemaling, and an Italian wooden box edged with a shell repeat motif—all incipient sources of inspiration. Granted, I bring the things I like to look on into my large closet, like a pack rat—but most people do surround themselves, in one way or another, with various patterns that they find pleasing.

Nature is a favorite source for peasant and sophisticated artist alike—the oak leaf and acorn, and the acanthus leaf and grape cluster have been repeated for over two thousand years

—remember the Greeks! Most peasant artists were stimulated by their daily surroundings. Fruit, flowers, grain, birds, leaves, animals are all found, over and over again, in the folk art of various countries. In Scandinavia, the farmer and his household spent the long, cold winters painting the chests they stored their possessions in, embroidering the clothes they wore, and carving the very spoons they used. Oddly enough—or perhaps it's proof that humans are not too different—the same motifs crop up in Russia, Spain, Italy, Norway, England and France. Daily life is not so varied, after all.

In European folk art, Christianity is a pervading influence. Hearts are beloved in Hungary and Czechoslovakia particularly —the Sacred Heart of Jesus. Grapes and ripe wheat, symbols of Communion, are favorites, and the pomegranate, another religious symbol, is even found in the far more sophisticated crewelwork of English ladies. Three fishes, entwined in a never-ending circle—symbolic of Christ (the fish), the Trinity (three), and Eternity (the circle)—are found from Italy and Portugal, the Slavic countries, Greece, all the way up through Norway and Denmark—wherever the traveling monks planted the seed. (This design is, wonderfully, in two quite disparate reference books of mine: *Folk Art of Europe* and *Symbols of the Church!*)

This art is, of course, the progenitor of American folk art in general and, most specifically, what is known as Pennsylvania Dutch. These settlers, of course, were not "Dutch" at all —they were *Deutsch*, or German, and they brought to Pennsylvania, along with their thrift and enormous affection for the land, the rich decorative tradition and love for color that flourished, then as now, in Germany and Switzerland. Earnest and industrious, they apparently believed, like my grandmother, that "the devil makes work for idle hands." Through them, the Sacred Heart, the tulip, the rose, and the birds and grapes came in the same ships, and underwent a distinctive and individualized transmutation in Penn's woods. There are, now, magnificent examples of their art in New York's Metropolitan Museum, in the Abby Aldrich Rockefeller Museum of Folk Art at Williamsburg, and in other museums in the United States. But these people didn't decorate their furniture, pottery, tin, barns, and bedding for museums—they did it for love. I suppose it is this very spontaneity that attracts me the most. In the midst of that harsh and forbidding wilderness, they surrounded themselves with charm and bright pattern. There is a poem, attributed to one Gulistan of Moslih Eddin Saadi, that reads:

> *If of thy mortal goods thou art bereft,*
> *And from thy slender store two loaves alone to thee*
>   *are left,*
> *Sell one, and with the dole*
> *Buy hyacinths to feed thy soul.*

I rather think that these settlers fed their souls the same way.

The German settlers of Lancaster and York counties in Pennsylvania were not alone in their craving for aesthetic pleasure as well as utility. The English of Connecticut and Vermont, Virginia and Maryland also made necessities beautiful as well as useful. Although the English have never been given to painting their furniture—only their pottery—they incised and inlaid decorative designs in their furniture made in the colonies long before the great cabinetmakers of Philadelphia, Baltimore, and Williamsburg produced their sophisticated masterpieces for the wealthy planters of pre-Revolutionary days. Wherever the colonists came from, they brought their heritage and adapted it to the native materials available in the raw land they tamed.

Public libraries are a rich source for books on Colonial and Pennsylvania Dutch—as well as other—designs. Many scholarly and exquisite books have been compiled on these subjects. They are a delight to pore over, even if you're not design hunting. In the bibliography I'm including some of my favorites, but I hope you will find some gems of your own.

I keep a folder of magazine clippings of designs that strike me as charming or usable, and I recommend this to you. I have clips from such diverse sources as a Nieman-Marcus pink-sale catalogue, and an ad from World Mining Yearbook—as well as needlepoint designs, scraps of wallpaper, and a last year's Christmas card. All of these are grist for the mill, some day.

Wallpaper, fabrics, book bindings, old silver, toleware, china, and pottery are also varied and rich storehouses of design. One of my students, who does perfect miniature work, traced a design from a favorite blouse and reproduced it on a metal cookie box. Another took a circular design from wallpaper left from her dining room and placed it on four sides and the top of a square tin box—then added a border that was a derivative of the central design. This spring I unearthed that most unattractive of necessities—the infant potty chair—for the smallest baby. Made of cheap pine, it was finished in a shiny yellow varnish, with a simpering decal of Mary and her lamb adorning the back. I painted this horror white, lifted the blue sprays of flowers from the bathroom wallpaper and made the back and sides bloom, added a ribbon of blue and green, and glazed it with a blue glaze. Although it is still a sow's ear and not a silk purse, it is far more attractive, and far less *noticeable* than it was before.

Fortunately, no one can pick a design for you—that's what

makes this kind of painting such an individual and delightful endeavor. One of my students asked, "Would you tell me if you hated my design?"

"No," I said.

"That's what I thought," she sighed, and went back to work. I'm not about to give you ten pages of designs to trace, and say, "This is it—look no further!" My *raison d'être* is to try to tell you how to translate your ideas into reality. I must say, though, that if your design is out of proportion to or incompatible with the piece you're doing, you're going to be terribly unhappy with it.

To paint a huge, elaborate bunch of fruit on a fragile candlestick would be just as unsuccessful as painting a hummingbird, life-size, in the center of a dining table; your design must be in proportion to your background. I also think it should be consistent in feeling. If your piece of furniture has curved French legs and delicate lines, the bold squareness of Pennsylvania Dutch tulips would not be a wise choice. Conversely, a sturdy, country pie safe doesn't lend itself to the delicate intricacy of a gold scroll. Try to let the design fit the piece and its purpose as well as the person who will be using it.

Close friends of ours recently had a new baby—and I had offered, before the infant was born, to do a piece of furniture for him or her. We bought a darling washstand, I had the base coat of white paint on it when a small son arrived. The washstand had a serpentine drawer, curved French legs, and a lyre-shaped towel bar that stood at the back edge of the top. I not only wanted it to be suitable for a small boy, but I wanted to create a piece that he could use as he grew. A dresser that would not be despised by an eleven-year-old budding athlete is not easy to do! I put bright red apples, hanging from brown branches with green leaves, on the drawers; on the cabinet door I put an apple tree, heavy with fruit. Another fruit-laden branch just fitted across the top, with a banner hanging from it that read, *"L'habit ne fait pas le moine!"*—the French equivalent of our "Clothes don't make the man." The drawers I lined with an Italian book endpaper that had a tiny, brown fleur-de-lis print.

His mother was pleased, and my own eleven-year-old boy was also admiring—so I figured I had pulled it off! Only time will tell.

Personalizing your pieces, and choosing the designs to suit their use is one of the reasons and motivations for antiquing and decorating with your own hands—no one else can do it your way. This touch cannot be bought. No matter how crude, it's original—and that is priceless. I love to slip mottoes into my work. On a sewing stand, "A stitch in time saves nine"; on a desk for my eldest daughter, *"Mieux vaut sagesse que richesse!"* (Wisdom is worth more than riches); for my middle daughter, who is reluctant to tackle anything that requires effort, *"Il n'y a pas de rose sans épines,"* (There is no rose without thorns). You don't have to use French—our own language is rich with proverbs and folk sayings. Nursery rhymes, lines of poetry, quotations from the Bible, lines from favorite hymns—all are appropriate. Around a mirror one might wreathe "Consider the lilies of the field . . ." or somewhere, surely, my favorite King Lear quotation, "How sharper than a serpent's tooth it is to have a thankless child!" (I have threatened to put this, in big, bold letters, around the bedroom ceilings of all my children.)

Often, too, the piece will suggest the decoration—and you can then let the whole effect grow in your mind. I must say, I prefer to do pieces for a specific person or place—these offer a chance for a special, individual touch that cannot be used on an item that is made to sell to the general public.

Once you know what you're going to do, there is then the imminent question of doing it. If you are experienced in painting, you'll feel comfortable doing what I do—plunging in freehand. Once I make up my mind, I may sketch out my ideas on a pad of newsprint—or, often, I take the paints and brush and paint it, in its entirety, on an old newspaper (this is one thing that is plentiful in every household!). Then I block out my design with chalk (plain, old, ordinary blackboard variety) on the piece, and begin. I do not, however, recommend this method for a first-timer.

Most of the people I have taught preferred to trace their designs and then transfer them to the project they were working on. Hopefully, all design sources will eventually be springboards to developing your own ideas—studied more as catalysts, and not copied verbatim. However, there is no sin in tracing a good design and transferring it to the piece you are decorating. I suggest that my students first trace the design on a piece of tracing paper and paint it in the colors they have planned to use. Although the background paint they have chosen probably won't be white, like the tracing paper, this gives them a chance to see the whole design as it will be—and they are more confident about the final execution on the finished drawer, or table top.

Do remember, too, that the background color will subtly change or intensify the colors in the design. If you have a green background paint, and are using red tulips, your red will be much redder than it is on a white background. (Remember complementary colors?) This may be just great—or you may want to dull your red after you get going, so it won't knock your eyes out. Then, too, the glaze will push all colors back and soften them—so don't let them be too dull in the beginning, or your work will simply fade away after it's glazed.

TRACING AND TRANSFERRING A DESIGN

When you're satisfied with your design choice, you are then ready to trace it as it is, and transfer it to your piece that now has the second coat of antiquing base paint. First, trace the design, with pencil or ball-point pen, on artist's or architect's thin tracing paper, available in art supply stores.

If your background paint is light in color, you then rub the back of the tracing paper (where the design is) with a very soft, flat drawing pencil—#3B, #4B, or #5B is best. This makes your tracing paper into a carbon. You may, if you wish, use carbon paper under your tracing paper—but this involves the hazard of slippage, particularly if you are working on a curved surface. Also, ordinary carbon paper has some wax or grease in it, often, and this may affect your paints. Pencil is easiest!

Fasten your design, pencil rubbing side down, onto your painted piece, using small pieces of *masking* tape. Do *not* use cellophane tape—it may lift the paint!

Once your design is carefully placed, go over every line of

it again, with either pencil or ball-point. In other words, retrace your design, thereby transferring it to its designated place on the object you're decorating. If you're putting the same design in several places on the piece (as the fronts of three or four drawers, or around a salad bowl), rub the back again with the soft pencil, to renew the carbon effect.

If your background paint is dark, or black, the procedure changes a bit. Tracing the design is the same, but—obviously—pencil will not make a mark on dull, black paint. Instead, you must rub the back of the tracing paper with a cake of *magnesium carbonate*. This is available in any drugstore for about 15 cents a cake. (If the druggist doesn't stock it, ask him to get it from his wholesaler. It's available in Evansville, Indiana—the heart of the Midwest—which makes me believe it should be available most places.) The magnesium carbonate will make a white carbon and transfer well on a dark or black background. The transferring process remains the same.

Often, you may wish to use part of a design, or split it, or lift parts of it for use on a side panel. This is perfectly legitimate, and often enhances your work. Again, be bold! Just because something was done as an entity by someone else doesn't mean that you can't change it to suit your own needs.

This spray of hearts and flowers could be a graceful beginning.

We can cut it here,

and put it on either side of a drawer, rather than in the middle. We can pick up parts of it, and use them on the sides:

Or, we can curl it up, and fit it on the front of a cedar chest.

You may also improvise, and extend a design—like so:

An adaptable motif may be curved, drawn out, separated, laid flat, or allowed to droop like hanging ivy with equal success. This is what the folk artists did with abandon, and we are free to do the same.

Whether you're attracted by a spray of roses and bluebells, a border of grapes, a meandering strawberry vine, or a stylized floral rosemaling or Pennsylvania Dutch design, the basic process of tracing and transferring it remains the same. Placement on the piece depends on you and how much decoration you want. One word—rather too much than too little. A painted and decorated piece of furniture is just that, and its charm and finesse lie in making your decorations outstanding and still a unified part of the whole. I enjoy picking designs so much that I seldom repeat myself—I'm always dying to see what the next one will look like on a different piece!

6

A TWISTED
TEARDROP

Freehand decoration—
The "stroke"—How to stripe

Scandinavian folk painting is freehand and free-flowing—albeit (with the exception of rosemaling) uneven. French furniture is elegant and quiet. Italian and Spanish majolica is gay and abandoned. Pennsylvania Dutch patterns are crude and stiff, with the charm of innocence. English delft is exquisitely intricate and civilized. The bond—the common denominator—between all these decorative styles, is what is known, in the trade, as the "stroke." Look carefully—you'll find a brush stroke, shaped like a teardrop, predominant in all these disparate pieces.

The stroke

can be twisted,

transposed,

combined,

flattened,

and curled into a scroll.

It is still *the stroke!*
        This design is built from it,

as is this one.

This basic brush stroke is made with the pointed watercolor brushes #3 and #8, and is accomplished by varying pressures. As you put the brush down on the paper or painted surface, you press hard, then lift slowly, turning the brush slightly in your hand as you lift. I find that I balance my hand with my little finger—the motion is controlled, more like lettering than straight painting.

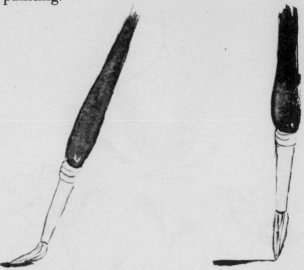

I suggest to all my students that they buy a bottle of poster paint —or use their children's—and practice this brush stroke until they get the feel of the special brush action and gain fluency in this manipulation of brush and paint.

The ¾-inch flat rigger is for big work. By turning the broad edge, and then the chisel edge, a lovely ribbon line flows forth.

Similarly, the brush may be used to make a teardrop.

When you have traced your pattern and transferred it to your piece of work, you will complete it best, more often than not, with this stroke. *Never* treat your pattern as inviolable—it's not a coloring book. If you've traced what is called a "polliwog border," for instance—

fill it in with the stroke, using the tracing as a guide. The lines are meant to be painted over, not just filled in.

The stroke lends itself to a variety of freehand borders: a twisted ribbon,

a scallop and teardrop,

a double scallop,

a ribbon and tassel,

or just a wavy line with tiny accents—dots, hearts, crosses—is attractive.

These need not be traced, when you are fluent enough with your brush. You may want to pick up a part of your design and, with this stroke, weave it into a border pattern.

Hearts and flowers, leaves and grapes, birds, shells, and intricate scrolls are all offshoots of *the stroke*. Keep practicing, and remember—the more you do, the more flowing your brush strokes become.

How to Stripe

Few touches put a more polished or professional look to a painted piece than a neat stripe—and few are, to my mind, more exasperating. This is probably a matter of temperament. I'm not given to precise, very careful, painstaking work—and this kind of accuracy is really the essence of a good stripe. Locally, we have a small, fine furniture factory that specializes in reproductions of beautiful Italian antiques. All of this furniture is hand-finished, and sold to a limited market at a justifiably high price. There are two men in this factory who stripe—this is all they've ever done. They were apprenticed as young men to a master striper, and they are highly skilled craftsmen—a premium on the market. So don't be discouraged if your first few stripes are not all that you might hope for. It takes a while, even for the pros.

I've tried a variety of brushes—in my unsteady and impatient hand!—and have had the greatest success with a *sword striper* or *Mack striper*—a special brush made just for striping. These can be bought, locally, in the art supply store or from a paint company outlet. This is what the master stripers in the factory use, and who should know better than they?

Mix your acrylic paint for striping in a small, separate container—the top from a hair-spray can, a medicine bottle, an ice-cube tray, a small jar—whatever is handy. Dilute your paint about half and half with matte varnish or polymer medium. To this, add water until the paint is the consistency of heavy cream. The paint should be thin enough to flow from the brush with ease. This paint, well covered, will not dry out, and can be used over a period of days, or even weeks.

Grasp the striping brush between your thumb and forefinger as you would a knife.

Have plenty of paint *in* the brush—dip it up to the ferrule. The basic principle in this technique is to let the brush do the work. A striping brush, with enough paint in it, will make a long, continuous stripe without additional paint. You simply pull the brush along, without pressure, letting the brush make the stripe. Your goal is not to lift the brush from beginning to end of the length of the stripe. If you have to stop for more paint, it *always* shows in the stripe—no matter how careful you are.

Before you begin to stripe, draw in all the lines with ordinary blackboard chalk and a ruler or straightedge. A stripe that goes at an angle or wavers is—at best—distracting. (At worst, ruinous!) For a wide stripe, outline both sides with the striping brush, then fill in the middle. I suggest, again, practice on a pad of newsprint, until you get the feel of the brush and the pulling action.

A striping guide—in effect, a straightedge that can be used as a steadying influence for your thumb—is easily made from an old yardstick. Cut the yardstick in two, and glue one piece on top of the other, with about ¼-inch of the long edge projecting on either side.

This guide, held with the left hand, can be put—like a ruler—by the chalked line. When it's lifted, it won't smear the freshly painted stripe. (Hold with the right hand, if you're a southpaw. I don't wish to force any leftie to stripe right-handed!) In comparison, a regular yardstick, held flat on the surface, often smears the wet stripe or line when picked up.

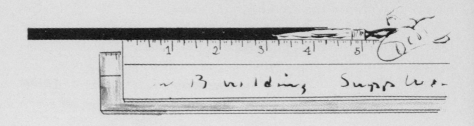

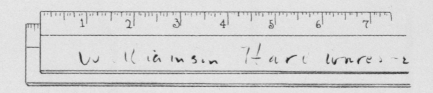

For perfect square corners, carry each line beyond the corner point (marked in chalk)—

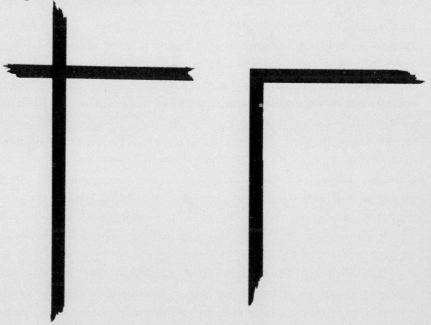

then, wipe off the overlapping extensions.

For a baroque panel, or other corner variations, bring your striping within an inch or two of the corner—

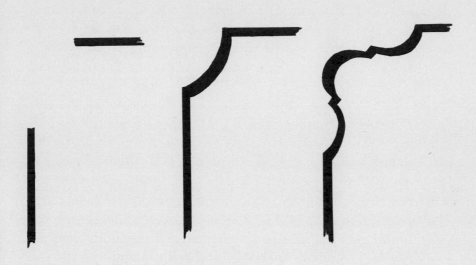

and connect the two stripes with a curve, or series of curves, using the striping brush.

Striping requires a steady hand, patience, and a certain amount of speed—he who hesitates wobbles! The acme of perfection is the moment when you grasp the striping brush and —whoosh!—pull out a perfect stripe with a single, confident stroke. Once the skill—for that's what it is—is mastered, it will give a remarkably finished look to your work. I've seen pieces that are striped only—no other ornament—and they are most sophisticated and effective. This is particularly true of Italian and French provincial furniture, so if you learn to stripe well, you'll be free to duplicate this charmingly simple provincial style.

After all your decorating is finished—including striping, borders, and proverbs—let it all dry thoroughly. Then give all a coat of matte varnish or polymer medium before you glaze or varnish. This is a protective coating that leaves a thin but tough plastic film over your work, and is a simple precaution against normal wear.

In some designs or settings, a spark of metallic paint adds a lot of zing to a decorative scheme. A couple of years ago, I bought a little washstand (my favorite piece!) in horrid condition. It had about seventeen coats of paint, and no drawer pulls, but the lines were French, and very appealing. I must have been feeling very Victorian (I'm a lover of Browning and Hardy, and was secretly Jane Eyre for several years in my youth, although my family would have preferred Elsie Dinsmore) because I could envision nothing more perfect for the washstand than a florid, Biedermeier treatment. Also, I was doing it for a charity auction, and it needed to be slanted to appeal to many buyers. I painted it a pale gray, and made it bloom with red and yellow roses, full blown. Around these bouquets I wreathed a dark, green-brown scroll, and overlaid the brown with liquid gold leaf that had a rosy cast. This gold leaf may be used like any paint, and it certainly adds a rich and elegant air. I found some fancy provincial hardware, and lined the drawers and little cupboard with a dark red, marbleized paper. The finished product was most successful, and the lady who bought it has it in her library. The gold-leaf touch, I felt, transformed it into a piece that would fit in any setting.

All gold and silver leaf must also be coated with matte varnish or polymer medium, or glaze will lift it as remover does nail polish. With this protective plastic coating, you may glaze over your metallic touches and they will still glow, softly, through the glaze.

When you are comfortable with these two techniques—the stroke, and the use of the striping brush—you're free to complete or duplicate most patterns. Give yourself some time and elbow room (not grease, this trip!) and your work will truly have a flair that is impossible to attain by just coloring within the lines. (Coloring books and elementary school art teachers destroy more creative talent than you can imagine.)

There is only one decorating technique that is absolutely *forbidden* in my classes and abhorrent to my mind!: the decal.

Better your work be primitive and a little messy than decal-slick, or cramped and dull.

7

THE
FLATTERING VEIL

Glazing and marbleizing

MY feminine, Southern mother always urged me—a born hat-hater—to buy hats with veils. They were, she avowed, so very flattering to any woman! So it is with glaze and a piece of furniture. An antique is old—venerable, ancient, mellow. But the piece you've been working on, now complete with base paint, decorations, and coat of matte varnish, is new—bright, fresh. Most antiques have a soft, warm patina of age (not dirt), the effect that you are about to duplicate with the aid of a brush, an old rag, and glaze. This is the part of the finishing process I always look forward to—particularly if I've been more harassed than usual by life and my various offspring. I purge myself of all inhibitions, hostilities, and urges to commit infanticide. Glazing is therapy—it's like finger painting. I put on my oldest jeans and sweat shirt and slosh away with abandon, wiping off here and adding there, until I have every crack and crevice properly aged, and all decorations enhanced with a thin coat of that wonder stuff—glaze.

Glaze is really nothing but varnish, slightly thickened, and tinted with oil paint. You can make your own by thinning satin varnish with a little turpentine, and adding enough artist's oil tube paint—burnt umber, raw umber, chrome green, or burnt sienna—to reproduce the epoch of antiquity that you are seeking. One company puts out a clear glaze base that you, have only to tint yourself. However, most companies have now chemically color-keyed glazes to base paint, and by using the pretested combinations, you are guaranteed that the finished product will match the sample you chose. I seldom mix my own glaze any more, unless I'm looking for an offbeat effect that I can't achieve any other way. Ready-mixed glazes come in brown, black, blue, yellow, red, green, gray, and blends that bridge these shades—what more could you ask for? A special glaze may be color-keyed to a particular base paint, but if you choose, you may cross over and use another that pleases you, or even apply two—one on top of the other. Certain finishes, particularly in the wood tones, call for two glazes to be used in sequence, and separately. I think blue over green, red over yellow, gray over russet, or various other combinations can be lovely on certain pieces. Don't feel that you are bound by what the back of the paint can says. If you want to mix things up, go ahead!

Back to the sloshing. When I'm ready to glaze, I find the oldest, rattiest bristle brush I have in the house—preferably one with stray hairs sticking to the sides in wisps, and no paint left on the handle. I get a pile of paper napkins, a wad of cheesecloth, an old terry-cloth towel, and an old toothbrush, put down lots of newspapers around the area, and I'm ready. (Do stir the glaze after it's just opened—the color tends to settle on the bottom as it does in regular paint.) Using my scruffy brush, I literally scrub the glaze over a section of my piece—working it into all cracks, crevices, and dents. Allowing a few minutes to let it set up, I then lift off the top of the excess with a paper napkin. With a towel or cheesecloth, I smooth the remaining glaze over the surface with long, sweeping strokes, leaving the edges darker than the center, and all imperfections well glazed.

This process eventually boils down to a matter of personal taste. I like glaze, and am liberal with it. Others take off as much as possible, leaving only a suggestion of color. I have one friend who very carefully paints her glaze on with a good brush, and leaves it as it is. You will have to experiment to discover the effect that pleases you.

Glaze doesn't have to be wiped off with a soft cloth. It can be removed with a dry brush, a sponge, coarse steel wool, fine steel wool, nylon net, or any other material that will leave the textural effect you're looking for. (I told you, it's just like finger painting!) Each of these materials creates a different surface, and this is fascinating. You can smooth the glaze with a soft cloth, dip a clean brush in clean mineral spirits and, by tapping the brush on the back of your hand and spraying the wet glaze with droplets of mineral spirits, create a tortoise-shell effect that's lovely. A dry sea sponge, patted on heavy, wet glaze, makes a stippled surface. A cellulose sponge, used the same way, leaves a different effect. A light plastic cleaner's bag, crumpled and dabbed on wet glaze, leaves a pattern not unlike marble. Burlap, wadded and dabbed, is another variation. Any nonabsorbent material can be used for manipulating the glaze. You'll probably discover your own tricks as you get into this. If you don't like your work, wipe it off and start again. Glaze doesn't set for about six hours, so you have plenty of time to remedy mistakes.

However—as with the decorating paint—once the glaze *is* dry, it's there to stay. Sandpaper is the only out. Once, I glazed half of a trunk as a demonstration for a class, and left it to dry. When I glazed the remaining half, I had a nice, dark line where the two sections met! I tried everything, including mineral spirits—and nothing fazed the glaze. Finally, I was able to sand it lightly and work over the spot until I was satisfied—but it was a job. So, if you are forced to stop, don't quit in the middle of the tabletop—a word to the wise is sufficient!

With two glazes, the first one must dry completely before the second is applied. You are, in essence, applying two veils of color—one over the other, like two layers of chiffon—and you don't want these mixed wet. Remember, too, that both glazes need not be applied in the same way. The first might be wiped with a soft cloth, the second with coarse steel wool—or the first dry-brushed, and the second stippled with a sponge. For tiny flecks, simulating worm holes, wait until the wiped coat of glaze is dry. Then, dip a clean brush in the same or a slightly darker glaze and tap it lightly on the back of your hand, spattering the surface with minute flecks of glaze. Instant age!

When glazing over decorations, leave less glaze there than on the plainer surfaces. In this way, your painting is high-lighted—rather as if it were in a picture frame.

Regardless of the technique you choose, be free and loose with your glaze. You can always wipe it off, and—again—your aim is a personal piece of work, not a factory-slick, mechanized finish.

When your glaze is dry, I advise one or two final protective coats of satin varnish—but not until Chapter 9.

GLAZING MATERIALS CHECKLIST

1 or 2 cans of antiquing glaze (one-half pint)
old bristle brush
paper napkins
cheesecloth
old terry-cloth towel or rag
old toothbrush
newspapers

Optional—for varied effects:

a clean, dry brush
1 sea sponge
1 cellulose sponge
coarse steel wool
fine steel wool
plastic cleaner's bag, or large sheet of thin plastic
nylon net

MARBLEIZING

Marbleizing is truly *trompe-l'oeil*, and is the only finish I am enthusiastic about that is not suitable for covering painted designs. Since you're faking real marble, you certainly don't want anything under the veining—or your fake is a flop. I have drawn panels, decorated them, and marbleized around them, and this is fun. But the surface that is to look like marble must be that—naught else.

This kind of finish is absolutely fascinating, and I've gotten so carried away with it that I even gave some thought to doing my kitchen cabinets until my husband remarked that this might be like cooking in my own tomb—a vision which has somewhat deterred me.

An off-white or dead-white undercoat is best for marbleizing. The base coat is prepared like any other, and sanded lightly to make a smooth eggshell surface. There are two methods or techniques that are possible—one using glaze, and one that involves painting veins directly into a coat of wet, white paint. They are equally satisfactory, so I can't recommend one above the other.

To marbleize with glazes, choose two different but compatible shades. Black and dark green, gray and russet, deep brown and red, or black and pale gray—nature's the limit, and marble, as you will discover, comes in an amazingly wide range of colors. If I were doing a marble with black and green veining I would first cover the entire surface with a very thin coat of green glaze. Then, while the glaze is still wet, I take a striping brush and begin to put in veining with black glaze on a section of the surface. From these veins, or streaks, I make—with a feather—the blurred streaks that are part of marble. After I've used the black glaze, I do the same with the green glaze, working through and intertwining the veins.

Unless you own a large duck, as I do, feathers may be hard to come by. (In the spring, when Benedict, our duck, cooperatively molts, the children and I save every feather for later use. If, in desperation, I need one and am out of stock, a swift footrace usually produces a couple—but this makes him mad and me tired. Molting is better.) If you don't own a duck—and few people do—may I suggest a turkey farm, poultry house, quill pen, or, if you go to the beach, gull feathers. Any one will do, but it must be fairly large.

As you work, you'll get the feel of making a deep spot of

color, a slender vein, and a broad feathered streak in an irregular pattern.

The veining in real marble is random; nature herself is often uneven, and your work must be also.

Marbleizing is, always, a wet-in-wet process, whether you work with glaze or wet paint. This floating of one color into another is what makes it so effective. Such subtle blends could never be achieved in a dry surface. In marbleizing with wet white paint, the method is basically the same. The surface you're doing gets a smooth coat of paint. Let the paint set for a few minutes—or even half an hour. Then, with a small pointed watercolor brush or a striping brush, begin veining, using artist's oils. Burnt umber, raw umber, burnt sienna, chrome green or terre vert, Indian red, lampblack, are all possible colors. When your veining is well begun, bring the feather into play. The oils will blur into the wet paint just as the glaze blurred

into the wet glaze, if you pull the paint out with the feather. How much to do is a matter of personal taste. If you're copying an actual sample, you'll naturally use that as a guide. I searched my husband's geochemical library for pictures of marble, and drew a blank. Then I went to the public library—no luck. Finally, in despair, I went to the local tile and monument company, and was able to beg some pieces of marble to work from. If you live near a large library, you shouldn't have nearly this much trouble, but it's fun to have a few actual samples in your hand.

It is not law that you marbleize an entire piece. The top of a table, for instance, may be enough—or the top of a small chest, or the back of a bench. For a real conversation piece, try marbleizing something that couldn't possibly be made of marble—a whole chest of drawers, or a small desk. Or combine marble with plain panels, like this—

I worked on this at an exhibit, open .to the public, and you wouldn't believe the people who were compelled to touch it to see if it really was marble!

Usually, when the veining is done, this is the final finish —glaze is not used. The only exception might be in an imitation of marble with a deep background color—green with black veins—when you might need to deepen the intensity of the green. Some natural marble has metallic flecks in it, and this can be faked with liquid gold leaf or the powdered gold that comes in small plastic tubes. Either one must be tipped in and feathered while the work is wet. On certain pieces, a golden glint is most effective.

As I write, I've been sneaking a few speculative looks at my little drafting table—it would certainly be unique in marble. One could even do a bathroom—if one tried. One could— well, do it and see. You may find yourself fighting the urge to marbleize everything!

Marbleizing Materials Checklist

2 cans antiquing glaze (one-half-pint size) in different but
compatible colors
1 striping brush, size #1 or #0
feathers
cheesecloth or rags

Optional:

1 small jar gold powder
    or
1 small bottle (about one-half ounce) liquid gold leaf

8

ANYTHING
WORTH DOING . . .

Lining and interior finishes—
Handling paper and cloth

I was raised in a household where proverbs flowed, on all occasions, like the gush of water from a mountain spring —or, at least, it seems so to me in retrospect. They included such pithy aphorisms as "Many hands make light work"; "God helps those who help themselves"; "Pretty is as pretty does"! But one of these many nutshell philosophies—most of them fallacious—apparently has embedded itself in my character forever: "Anything worth doing is worth doing well." If I'm sewing, I cannot—even in this day of zigzag and multitudinous, interchangeable cams—bring myself to put a hem in a dress on the machine—or to finish the neck or sleeves with machine stitching, for that matter. I was taught fine, hand finishing and I cannot escape it—much as I would like to. The same compulsion has me by the throat when I'm working on a piece of furniture. If the insides of the drawers, shelves, cabinets, and even the back are not finished to suit me, I'm not satisfied.

82

This may seem an insane obsession to some. What difference does it make, if the insides of the drawers are decorative, as long as they're clean? No difference, really. I am simply unwilling to undertake all the trouble, work, and loving effort that go into antiquing and decorating a piece of furniture, and not have it finished—so to speak—in the round. It gives me pleasure to open a drawer and see the contrast of a lining. I like to *know* that the back is sealed against dust. Call it the curse of the perfectionist or whatever you will—this is the way I finish all furniture. There is one valid, logical reason for doing this, besides a personal aberration. Finishing the interior seals old dirt *in*, as well as protecting from without. I always feel that if something has stood in a warehouse, barn, or worse for years, it has absorbed a good deal of dirt that cannot be washed away, and this is the only way I know to defeat it. Then, too, no musty smells, no splinters—everything is fresh again. (My friends, who know how I despise housework, will be holding their sides when they read this, as it is in direct contradiction to my apparent character. No doubt, my housekeeping suffers because I'd much rather be painting than dusting!)

Drawers, shelves, cupboards, and what have you may be finished with a lining of paper or cloth, or may be painted, decorated, and glazed. I always, as I paint a drawer, paint not only the front that faces the world but the two short sides of the

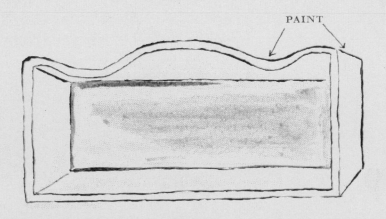

PAINT

rectangle that slide in, and the top edges of all four drawer faces, including the back.

Often, I'll prime the inside as well as the outside, even if I'm going to line it. The primer gives a sealing coat, and leaves a smooth finish for glue as well as paint.

I then forget the interior until everything else is done. Paint, decorate, and glaze the outside, and let it all dry. (If you don't glaze first, you cannot avoid smearing some on the interior—unless you have the patience of a saint!—as I, obviously, have not.)

If a drawer has a cracked bottom, or splinters, or a large, protruding nail that can't be moved, the best solution is a false bottom. This can be cut from heavy poster board, mat board, 1/16-inch masonite (or whatever your building supply man has to suggest), finished, and slipped in after the sides are complete. (Don't put it in beforehand—you may never get it out!)

Painting interiors is most attractive, particularly if you choose a contrasting color. Use two coats, just as you have done

on the exterior. Usually, I decorate the inside with a repeat pattern—a simple bud, a cross-stitch X, a tiny fleur-de-lis—anything that is done quickly with one or two brush strokes. Each drawer might be labeled inside for contents—socks, shirts, sweaters. Use the same decorating paints that you've used on the outside.

A coat of matte varnish, glaze that suits the interior color, and you're ready to finish inside and out with varnish. This kind of finish is particularly charming on a piece for a child, where durability is as necessary as beauty. I did my baby's washstand like this.

Lining with paper or cloth opens up a whole new field of pattern, texture, and colors. Since I started this bit, I've become an avid collector of unusual paper—other than wallpaper, which is, of course, an obvious choice. Reproductions of old book endpapers, wrapping paper, Japanese printed rice paper, Chinese tea paper that comes in gold and silver—all may be used for lining and are marvelous. I have my eye out for papers whenever I go out of town, and haunt out-of-the-way art galleries, searching. Some art galleries handle oddments like lovely papers, or unusual prints, along with their paintings and sculpture. Book endpapers can be bought locally—and I imagine most art supply stores or job printers have a selection of unusual paper that may be ordered, by the sheet, if you ask to see it. Watch museum boutiques at Christmas—or any time. They often carry unusual wrapping papers.

Reproductions of old prints, often sold for very little, would be fascinating lining paper. Old black-and-white woodcuts of herbs, for instance, in a kitchen piece—particularly one that you had already decorated with herb designs. Consider old maps, or ship drawings, in the drawers of a desk. Prints of cats and kittens in something for a child might be an incentive for neatness—the child would get a thrill every time he opened a drawer!

Wallpaper, of course, is excellent. My only objection is that most really lovely papers have to be ordered, by the roll, and

aren't available off the shelf. It is seldom necessary to use a whole roll of wallpaper for one piece of furniture, and the cost goes up. Be sure, if you pick a vinyl paper, to buy the special vinyl paste along with it. Nothing else will glue vinyl securely.

French furniture—some of the great armoires that stand, still, in some Parisian hotels—was always lined with cloth. Here again, search for the unusual—toile, chintz, calico, burlap, even velveteen could be used. (Remember when the walls of all well-built houses had a canvas lining?) The main consideration in choosing material is to avoid a print that has a straight-line pattern. Fabric has a tendency to pull on the bias after it's wet with glue, and trying to keep a pattern line true to the drawer edge could be a maddening struggle. Better to find an allover print that doesn't require a T square to make it look right. I love to use calico—it seems so right with primitive furniture, and it's very easy to handle. Sometimes decorators will have a sale of their out-of-date samples—don't miss it. You don't need an entire bolt of fabric to line a small piece, but often the most attractive fabrics come only by the bolt.

The mechanics of lining with either paper or cloth is virtually the same. The necessary tools are:

> White glue, synthetic resin wallpaper adhesive, or cellulose wallpaper paste (not wheat)
> A clean bristle brush—1″ or 2″
> A wide putty knife
> Sharp scissors
> Yardstick and/or ruler
> Pencil
> Old newspapers

An oblong or square drawer or shelf presents no problem. For the drawer, mark off your lining material with pencil, and cut the bottom first—allowing about ¼-inch extra all the way around. Then measure and cut each side separately, measuring depth exactly but allowing ½-inch overlap at the corners.

I use ordinary white household glue, diluted about 1/3 with hot water, and spread it with the paintbrush. The synthetic resin-type or cellulose wallpaper paste that mixes and dries clear is fine, but it must be mixed in a quantity that is often too large for my needs. Wheat paste isn't on my list, because it attracts bugs—and who wants bugs?

I use the thinned glue and brush on cloth, just as I do on paper. However, my teen-age daughter, Graeme—who now does most of my lining for me—has evolved her own crafty method that I'll pass on to you. She squeezes the glue on the fabric straight, right out of the bottle. Then, dipping a sponge in hot water, she spreads the glue, diluting it as she spreads. Works like a charm!

After the glue is spread evenly and completely on the back of each measured and cut piece (work on the old newspapers, and do one drawer at a time), put the piece in place on the wood and, with the broad edge of the putty knife, smooth it flat —working out any wrinkles or air bubbles. Don't worry about any excess glue that appears—either kind will dry clear, and you'll never see it.

A drawer with a serpentine curve, a trunk top, or a round

box are not quite as simple. The easiest approach is to cut a pattern or template out of old newspaper. Place the bottom of the drawer or box on the newspaper and draw around it with a pencil. Cut out this drawing to make your pattern, and cut the bottom lining paper by this template. Drawer or box sides may be measured and cut according to the depth and length. The only way I know to cut a pattern for a curved trunk top is, again, to make a newspaper template and use this as the pattern for the lining paper.

If you have to piece—and I often do—go ahead. It won't ever show, once the glue is dry—particularly with an allover print. Piecing is almost essential in a trunk, because few papers come as wide as most trunks are.

I've been meaning to talk about trunks ever since Chapter 1, and I'm just getting around to it. There is nothing difficult about a trunk—it's just big. Many old trunks are wood, and should be handled as any wooden piece. We have a peculiar species around here—at least, peculiar to me, as I've never seen this type before. The frame of the trunk is wood, covered with metal. The curved staves or bindings across the top are wood, held in place with elaborately chased metal hasps. The two center sections of this metal on the trunk top and down the front are richly embossed in a *repoussé* fashion. Odd, but lovely! My own theory—as yet unsubstantiated by any local historian (there is only one of any note)—is a drummer, who came through the Middle West with a wagon and sheets of tin, pierced and embossed in various designs. Local itinerant carpenters must have flocked to the wagon, purchased the tins they fancied, and made trunks and pie safes from them for strictly local trade. If any knowledgeable antiquarian can give me any more information, I'd be delighted.

If you have such a trunk—and the type may be more generally known than I think—treat it as any metal piece. Because I think the *repoussé* work is so unusual, I highlight it by rubbing it with a metallic leaf wax before I apply the glaze. This brings out the depth of the embossing, and still, it doesn't knock your eye out.

Any trunk lends itself to treatment as a bride's or dower chest. The Swedish painters did these chests superbly, with bouquets of flowers twined usually around the year—say, 1797— the chest was made, and this is the feeling I have tried to recapture on my own. Line it as you would a drawer, and if you have the tray, line that too—and hang on to it! Trunk trays are mighty rare these days.

Someone is bound to ask, now, about the preglued plastic papers that come, ready to apply, from the ten-cent or hardware stores. They're great for use on kitchen shelves or closets, and you may certainly use them for lining drawers if you choose. I don't, because I feel the patterns and colors are limited, and I find them difficult to smooth out in small areas.

Once my lining—any lining, except velveteen— is dry and

well glued, I give it all one coat of satin varnish. When this is dry, it's invisible, and it seals the paper against dampness and grease. When varnished, a drawer or shelf can be wiped off with a damp cloth—a wise voice from my youth whispers, "Cleanliness is next to Godliness"!

9

THE FINISHING
TOUCHES

Varnishing, hardware,
false bottoms and sides, waxing

THIS IS, in a manner of speaking, the end of the
trail—the pot of gold at the end of the rainbow, or the last mile,
depending on how sore and tired you are! (Once, I was in such
pain, I was sure I had a severe arthritis in my left shoulder, and
not just my simple bursitis that flares up now and again. I
couldn't imagine what I'd done to irritate the joint. Then it
dawned on me that I'd just spent hours sitting on the floor,
painting a desk, leaning on my left arm while I wielded the
brush with my right! If you have a few sore muscles, don't be
surprised or alarmed.) Your work is now complete, with the
exception of this—the finishing touch—and you should be sitting back proud and pleased, admiring as you varnish. (I always admire! This isn't vain—even though my Calvinist up-
bringing whispers that it is. It's simple pride and pleasure in
accomplishment.)

Varnish is, to me, a very necessary final step. It gives all
your work a tough coating that will protect it from wear, nicks,

scuffs, water, Super Stuff (that gooey plastic my children are constantly dripping about the house), and all the various hazards of living. There are paint company instructions that allow you to omit it—but I'll be darned if I'm going to advise you to create something lovely and then let it be ruined in six months by a careless or unavoidable scratch. Two coats of varnish take, at best, two or three more days' drying time—and it's a small investment for the resulting protection.

I always use a satin varnish (brand names differ, but if you ask the clerk, he'll tell you) unless I'm doing a piece that will be outside in the weather. For this, I brush on a first coat of spar varnish (the kind recommended for boat decks) and use satin varnish as my second coat—steel-wooling between coats. This combination is a neat trick. If, for instance, you have a table top that will have hard wear, you may put a first coat of this *very* glossy super-tough varnish over your work. The second coat of satin takes out all the gloss, and you have your cake and are eating it, too! Now, I am aware that the paint industry is making revolutionary advances in the chemistry of paint, varnish, and all finishes. The new polyurethane varnishes are excellent, and I try any new product that is generally recognized to be superior to an old standby. So, if you want to use a new type of varnish finish, do—be daring! Polyurethane, plastic, whatever—just so long as it's a dull, satin finish. This satin varnish finish gives any piece the soft glow that is part of a hand-rubbed finish—a warm patina that is beautiful.

Varnishing holds no terror. Always use a fresh or, ideally, a new brush—but keep it a special brush, used only for this purpose. Do your varnishing in daylight, if possible and—preferably—not in a cloud of dust! Wet varnish *does* pick up dust particles easily. Some manufacturers specify a "dust-free room" —but if you can find one, I wish you'd let me know where it is. Possibly at Cape Kennedy, Cal Tech, or M.I.T.— but the average house, if mine is anywhere near normal, is hardly dust-free. Nevertheless, I usually work inside the house, rather than on the terrace, where more dust is apt to be blowing around. Varnish, like any form of paint in a can, should be stirred gently to reincorporate ingredients that may have settled on the bottom. But don't stir varnish with vigor—bubbles form, won't escape, and you'll be brushing them on like shaving cream.

The whole trick in doing a smooth coat is to let the varnish *flow* from your brush—the smoother the stroke, the better. Tip your brush on the can, of course—don't apply varnish with a dripping brush. But don't try to milk every drop out of the brush before you dip again. Keep as full a brush as possible. After you've brushed the entire surface *with* the grain of the wood, (even though you can't see it), then crosshatch your strokes, going across the grain.

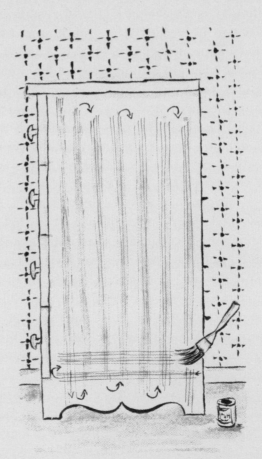

This fills in any tiny spots that you may have missed, and ensures an even, smooth coat. Brush strokes don't show in varnish, and it's difficult to see if the surface is covered evenly, unless you get down and squint across the wet surface, with the light just right!

I use two coats of varnish—for the same reason that I line drawers. I just feel better about it. As most varnish has a drying time of about 12 hours, one could varnish at night and apply the second coat the next morning. If you *can* wait longer, do—give the first coat a good chance to harden in a warm, dry room. Rub down the first coat with a very fine steel wool before the second coat goes on. When the second coat is dry, rub it down with the same grade steel wool, gently. This simply eliminates any chance of a hard gloss, and makes the surface like satin to the touch.

If you have too much gloss, or if you prefer, you may rub the varnish down with rottenstone and paraffin oil, the way old-fashioned, fine cabinetmakers did all their handwork. (Both may be bought in most paint stores.) Rottenstone is a form of pumice, and it works much faster than steel wool, so be careful. You only want the surface to be dull, not to disappear. This mixture will take out any chance particles of dust, or other possible imperfections in the surface, and is a valuable technique to have in your repertoire.

When your last coat of varnish is dry, you're ready to put on the hardware, restore hinges, rehang doors, and put the whole puzzle back together again. With luck, your husband may be handy and able to help you. Mine is not fond of this type of endeavor (that old left-handedness raises its ugly head!), but my twelve-year-old son is great with his hands, and does most of this for me. Recruit any help you can.

You may find that two coats of paint and varnish have made the door a hairsbreadth too big and it won't fit. Don't panic! Just sand, carefully, the top and bottom edges, and the side edge where the hinges go, until the door slips in. These edges aren't noticeable, anyway, and the removal of even one coat of varnish may be all that's needed.

Hardware I'm difficult about. A bad choice can shatter the best-laid design. Generally, the original hinges may be used again, with new screws—unless you can find the same size on the market. Many times, drawer and door pulls are missing, broken, or unbelievably ugly. White porcelain pulls, or plain round wooden ones, painted and finished exactly like the drawers, are often the best solution. They don't stand out and detract from the decoration, and they are in harmony with the mood or age of the furniture. (Too fancy, too shiny, cheap imitation hardware is the worst solution!)

If you are lucky enough to have the original brasses, rejoice! They may be black as pitch, but they're treasures. Soak them overnight in straight household ammonia, or for about 15 minutes in the following solution:

    1/3 cup household ammonia
    1/3 cup baking (not washing) soda
    1/3 cup vinegar
    1 cup very hot water

(This formula was given me by one of my students, and I'm eternally grateful.) Fifteen minutes is enough, because this is powerful stuff. After the brasses have soaked, remove them and scrub them with an old toothbrush to get the black out of the indentations. Polish, finally, with a good brass polish, and you'll be delighted.

Sometimes, the original pulls are extant, but they're not brass, or they're not uniform. On my baby's washstand, four of the pulls were the same, and some character had replaced the fifth with another type that was also rather charming. The original four had been a type of silver finish—the fifth looked brass. Since I liked them all, and I thought this oddity added interest, I rejuvenated them to a uniform finish by rubbing all with a pewter metallic wax. This wax comes in almost every metal imaginable, and is simply great! Once it's on, it's like a replating job, and each shade reproduces the color and sheen of the original metal. When the wax is dry (a few minutes),

you may spray your pulls with a clear plastic spray (comes in a can)—again, insurance against wear. These pulls have been in hard use for two years now, and there's not a sign of fading —they look, to me, like well-rubbed pewter.

I mentioned false bottoms when I was involved with lining, but I'll say again that they're a very nice finishing touch, even if you're not lining. The little cabinets in washstands, or big ones in buffets, may also need false sides—as well as a false bottom—if the interior has been left in the rough. These, too, may be made from poster board, illustration board, or mat board, covered with lining, and tacked in place—or cut to measure from masonite (at the mill where you buy it) and nailed in.

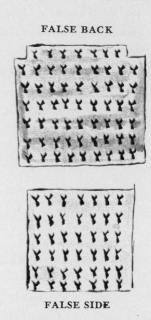

FALSE BACK

FALSE SIDE

This is a refinement that may not be at all necessary—it depends on the piece. In an old pie safe or Welsh cupboard, for instance, where the simplicity of the open interior is in keeping with the exterior, I like the look of the tool marks on the shelf supports. If the interior is not quaint or hand-done—just ugly— it is simple to mask the unattractive part.

Back to varnish! After the second coat of satin varnish is dry, and rubbed down to a lovely sheen, I put a coat of good paste wax all over the outside of the finished piece. (If any drawers are sticking, rub the sliding edges with a cake of paraffin—the kind used in jelly and jam making.) Professional house painters tell me that a month—or at least two weeks—should elapse between the final coat of varnish and the wax. This, apparently, allows the varnish to set hard. Otherwise, some moisture might be present that could cause trouble later on. I haven't always waited that long—because I'm impatient, and I couldn't!—but I suggest that it's prudent. Buff the wax with a soft cloth or towel to—guess what?—a soft glow, and you're through. (I have a penchant for a wax that smells like lemon verbena—might as well delight another sense!) Your work is finished. You may now call in all your family, friends, and chance acquaintances—who will promptly faint dead away with delight!

You have (to paraphrase Keats, who appreciated loveliness in any form)—I'm sure—created a thing of practical beauty and—I hope—a joy forever. Now, what's next?

CHECKLIST OF STEPS—FROM START TO PERFECT FINISH

1. Sand all rough spots. Remove hardware. Make any necessary repairs.
2. Strip old paint off, if necessary.
3. If metal, treat for rust.
4. Prime coat, using liquid sander to soften the old finish—if the piece hasn't been stripped. Optional.
5. Sand lightly.
6. Put on one or two coats of antiquing undercoat paint. Sand lightly between coats with extra-fine finishing paper.
7. Decorate, if desired.
8. Cover *all* decoration (if using acrylics) with a coat of acrylic matte varnish, including any metal leaf.
9. Glaze.

10. Line drawers or shelves.
11. Give piece, including lining material, one or two coats of satin varnish.
12. Rub the exterior varnish down, not the lining, with rottenstone and paraffin oil, or a very fine steel wool.
13. Replace the hardware.
14. After a month, or at least two weeks, wax with a good paste wax, and buff to a soft, dull finish.
15. Enjoy the fruits of your labor!

10

A PIG IN A POKE

Pitfalls and bargains

A FEW words of wisdom from a perennial pig-in-a-poke buyer. (I prefer to think of myself as an innocent, but I fear this is a rationalization.) If you've been bitten by this antiquing bug, and are now pawing through junk shops, hanging around auctions, and visiting the wrecking company weekly, you're eventually going to be taken—how badly depends on the dealer, and your own greed. If you've been looking for something *just like this*, and the proprietor can sense your delight, and he *knows* there's something wrong with the piece—he's not about to tell you. He's found his pigeon, you're blinded by excitement and covetousness—and there it is. If it's any comfort, I can't believe that there's anyone embroiled in this kind of pastime who hasn't, at some time or other, bought a pig in a poke and been swindled.

An old pie safe was my most recent undoing. I had been dying for one for months, and there it stood! I looked at it, went home and thought about it, went back to the shop, looked at it again—and, delighted, bought it. I did notice, as I wrote out the check, that some booby had painted the tin panels with copper metallic paint, and I groaned inwardly at the thought of stripping off that paint—but that was all I groaned about. I stored it carefully in the basement of my husband's office, and didn't look at it again for months. When the time was ripe, I brought it home, took the doors off, got out the paint stripper— and discovered who the booby was! I had been taken. The tin beneath the paint was all rusted. I went ahead and stripped all the panels, stopped the rust, and then began to try to find a way out of this fiasco. I tried flat black, steel wool, chromium cleaner, a gilding wax. Finally, after wasting literally hours and hours of work, I decided I could only paint the tin the color of the wood and be content. The result is not a disappointment, but I had visions of that tin glowing like pewter, and that can never be. I shall not go hunting again without a pocketknife that can make a small exploratory scrape through the paint on tin panels, or through coats of cherry stain to the poplar underneath and, I hope, pierce a few other dealer-made deceptions. You have, in your searching, a perfect right to open the poke before you buy the pig!

When you go hunting, wear your oldest clothes, and take the children in the rags you've put aside for the Good Will. There was never a successful dealer who was a fool, but I think this helps keep the price within talking range. Do bargain— most dealers are used to it, and take you for an idiot if you swallow their first price.

Beware of auctions! You can get bargains, but you may get carried away. Our busiest local auctioneer plays me like a violin, and I get so excited that I find myself bidding on something I don't want, never did want, and have no use for—I enter a state not unlike a hypnotic trance. My mother, a lady of similar temperament and enthusiasm, once came home from an auction proudly bearing a lead statue of a nude woman with a clock in her stomach. She swore it was a purchase born of hysteria. She had meant to bid on a cut-glass bowl, nodded her head at the wrong moment, and got the clock instead! We lived with it for

years, rather like a penance, since she couldn't even give it away.

Auctions are exciting, but hazardous.

In any case—whether you luck onto your heart's desire, or a lead Venus with a barometer instead of a navel—this kind of shopping is fascinating. Nine times out of ten you will get what you've bargained for, and the tenth time—well, you're not alone. And, with antiquing, imagination, and elbow grease, you may even rescue your mistake.

11

FOOTWORK
AND INGENUITY

What paints and decorates well—
Sources of supply

Although auctions and junk shops aren't the only places to make great finds, this kind of shopping can't be done on the telephone. I sometimes call the Good Will, the Salvation Army, or my favorite secondhand store to see if they have anything that is even close to the piece I'm looking for—but I have to *see* it to know whether I want it or not. If they have nothing of that description, it just saves me a trip. Certainly, in the line of furniture, any of these could be a fine, usable choice.

Welsh cupboard, or safe
Washstand
Cedar chest or blanket chest
Dry sink
Wardrobe
Chest of drawers
Chairs
Round table—pedestal tables are nice

Trunk
Golden oak *anything*

Several of my students have started with cedar chests. They're not confusing, as they have good, straight lines, and large, smooth surfaces for decorating. Charming bars can be done from dry sinks—the metal lining in the top is ideal.

My favorite washstands, cupboards or safes, or round tables are not difficult either.

Chairs can be tricky, but many of my class members have worked on them with excellent results.

If you hear of any church pews being on the market—grab them! They aren't hard to work with, and make great patio or garden benches.

Unfinished furniture is not to be overlooked. There are many charming pieces being made today, with good lines that would paint and decorate well. In this market, you get what you pay for—so be sure your choice is sturdy, and solidly made, and you'll be pleased.

If you don't want to plunge in with something big, try a bread box for your kitchen, or a half barrel to be put on the terrace, or beside the fireplace as a wood basket. (Casters on the bottom of a barrel make life easier, leave backs unstrained, and floors unscratched.) Wastebaskets, milk cans (for umbrellas), sugar buckets, mirror frames are all small items that decorate well. One of my friends and students worked on a breadboard for six weeks—every time she came to class, she'd paint a new design on it, stand back, look at it, and wipe it off at the end of the session. I began to wince every time I saw that darned board under her arm! She *finally* finished it—beautifully—on the last night, and she had honestly learned a great deal by just experimenting, over and over, on that board.

I love to do galvanized ware—buckets, washtubs, and something called a "coal bushel" that the hardware store has to order from the wholesaler for me. This is a round, two-bushel container with side handles, and a bottom fluted like a melon mold. I'm advised that people who have coal stoves use these graceful buckets to carry their coal into the house from the shed or cellar. Whatever they are used for, they're marvelous to paint and decorate.

They may be used to hold magazines, wood, toys, flowers, or to serve as wastebaskets. My sister-in-law uses hers by the fireplace for kindling chips. I've done these for very special Christmas presents, and filled them with jars of strawberry jam, pickled peaches, watermelon pickle, chili sauce, and anything else I'd managed to put on the shelves during the summer. Sounds a little Red Ridinghoody, but they've always made a hit.

Christmas, of course, is a perfect time to display your skills. An inexpensive galvanized bucket, painted and decorated, makes a beautiful and very personal gift without a huge cash outlay. I've even done a great big wastebasket for a favorite kitchen, using colors appropriate for the recipient.

Toy buckets for little ones, lunch boxes decorated with painted ribbons and the names of the recipients for the grade-school set, personalized bulletin boards for teen-agers are welcome gifts. As I love Christmas, I could rave on—but these hints should stimulate your thinking.

SOURCES OF SUPPLY

I have deliberately, from the very beginning of this book, avoided mentioning any basic need that even smacked of the exotic, or order-by-mail-only. (A burned child fears the fire!) In the past, I've gone to various local suppliers and asked for something out of the ordinary—and received no answer but a slack jaw and a look of pained disbelief. If they've never heard of it, it doesn't exist, and that's that! I wanted to spare you the frustration, possible harsh words, and wasted gasoline. Anything specifically mentioned in the preceding pages can be bought from any paint store, hardware store, or art supply house. There are few communities of over 5,000 that don't have all of these, or aren't close to a larger town that will supply the missing link. My husband's mother is from Prestonsburg, Kentucky, a small town deep in the mountains of eastern Kentucky. I found antiquing kits in the Prestonsburg ten-cent store—so I know whereof I speak.

For a few elusive items, or for something you can't find locally, here are some large supply houses that should be able to fill your needs.

Artist's supplies: For acrylic paints in tubes, sabeline brushes, striping brushes, polymer medium, and a complete line of *all* artist's supplies, write to:

> A. Langnickel, Inc.
> 115 West 31 Street
> New York, N.Y. 10001   catalog 25¢

or

> Arthur Brown & Bro., Inc.
> 2 West 46 Street
> New York, N.Y. 10036   catalog free

> Favor Ruhl and Watson Company
> 121 South Wabash St.
> Chicago, Illinois 60603   catalog free

Professional finishing supplies: Perhaps the most complete house in the United States for these is:

> H. Behlen and Bro., Inc.
> 10 Christopher Street
> New York, N.Y. 10014   catalog 25¢

Hardware: Any type of hardware, including tools, drawer pulls, knobs, hidden springs, etc., may be ordered from:

> Albert Constantine & Son, Inc.
> 2050 Eastchester Road
> Bronx, N.Y. 10461   catalog 25¢

Marble: Marble may be ordered from:

> Door Store of Washington
> 3140 M Street N.W.
> Washington, D.C. 20007   catalog 50¢

or

> Vermont Marble Co.
> 61 Main Street
> Proctor, Vermont 05765

Unpainted furniture: For attractive and authentic reproductions of early American furniture, unfinished, try:

> Cohasset Colonials
> Cohasset, Massachusetts 02025   catalog 25¢

or

> Yield House
> Dept. 217
> North Conway, New Hampshire 03860
>   catalog free

Unfinished traditional reproductions: Louis XVI, Empire, Regency and Provincial—chairs and other furniture—available through:

> Door Store of Washington
> 3140 M Street N.W.
> Washington, D.C. 20007   catalog 50¢

Patterns: If you would like early American or Provincial patterns already printed and ready to trace, these were drawn at my suggestion. (I get no revenue from them, or from anything else mentioned here. But I am familiar with these designs; they're color-keyed to the palette I use, and they're very nice.) The Country Store also handles a complete list of acrylic paints and the brushes for decorating in a kit form, and is a source for new trunk handles—if you need them. Just write:

> Country Patterns
> Newburgh Country Store
> Newburgh, Indiana 47630

All basic supplies: If you live out of reach of a hardware or paint store, there's always the "wish book"—Sears, Roebuck and Company. The Sears catalog lists a complete line of paints, brushes, primers, sandpaper, mineral spirits, antiquing kits, varnish and all the other aforementioned supplies. (They do advertise an antiquing kit with a latex paint as a base—but we'll skip that.) I have used Sears products, and they are all that they should be. The address I have is:

> Sears, Roebuck and Company
> Chicago, Illinois 60607

Good hunting!

BIBLIOGRAPHY

History and Design:

BEDFORD, JOHN. *Delftware.* New York, Walker & Company, 1966.

BOSSERT, HELMUTH TH. *Folk Art of Europe,* Translated by Sybil Moholy-Nagy. New York, Frederick A. Praeger, 1964.

FÉL, EDIT; HOFER, TAMÁS; K-CSILLÉRY, KLARA. *Hungarian Peasant Art.* Budapest, Hungary, Kossuth Printing House, Corvina Budapest, 1958.

KAUFFMAN, HENRY. *Pennsylvania Dutch American Folk Art.* New York, Dover Publications, Inc., 1964.

KORF, DINGEMAN. *Dutch Tiles.* Translated from the Dutch by Marieke Clark. New York, Universe Books, Inc., 1964.

LICHTEN, FRANCES M. *Folk Art of Rural Pennsylvania.* New York, Charles Scribner's Sons, 1946.

LIPMAN, JEAN, & MEULENDYKE, EVE. *American Folk Decoration.* New York, Oxford University Press, 1951.

PLATH, IONA. *The Decorative Arts of Sweden.* New York, Dover Publications, Inc., 1966.

SABINE, ELLEN S. *American Antique Decoration*. Princeton, N.J., D. Van Nostrand Co., Inc., 1956.
————. *American Folk Art*. Princeton, N.J., D. Van Nostrand Co., Inc., 1958.
————. *Early American Decorative Patterns and How to Paint Them*. Princeton, N.J., D. Van Nostrand Co., Inc., 1962.

Practical Advice:

BRUSHWELL, WILLIAM, ed. *Goodheart-Willcox's Painting and Decorating Encyclopedia, A complete library of professional know-how on painting, decorating, and wood finishing in one easy-to-use volume*. Homewood, Illinois, The Goodheart-Willcox Company, Inc., 1964.
DANIELS, GEORGE. *The Awful Handyman's Book*. New York, Harper & Row, 1966.
DENISTON, G. L. *The Science of Modern Wood Finishing*. Dayton, Ohio, Research Press, Inc., 1949.
GROTZ, GEORGE. *Antiques You Can Decorate With*. Garden City, N.Y., Doubleday and Co., Inc., 1966.
————. *The Furniture Doctor*. Garden City, N.Y., Doubleday and Co., Inc., 1962.
————. *Instant Furniture Refinishing and Other Crafty Practices*. Garden City, N.Y., Doubleday and Co., Inc., 1966.
HUNT, PETER. *Peter Hunt's How-to-do-it Book*. New York, Prentice-Hall, Inc., 1952.
————. *Peter Hunt's Workbook*. New York, Ziff-Davis Publishing Co., 1945.
JENSEN, LAWRENCE N. *Synthetic Painting Media*. Englewood Cliffs, N.J., Prentice-Hall, Inc., 1964.
MAYER, RALPH. *The Artist's Handbook of Materials and Techniques*. Revised Edition. New York, The Viking Press, 1963.

GLOSSARY OF TERMS

Acrylic matte varnish—See matte varnish.

*Acrylic paint—*Artist's tube paint, a combination of pigment or color and a synthetic acrylic resin emulsion; sold under various brand names as Liquitex, Shiva Acrylics, New Masters, Weber, Hyplar, Aquatec, and others. Water-soluble.

*Acrylic resins—*Synthetic resins of excellent color and clarity used in both emulsion and solvent-based paints.

*Alkyd—*A synthetic resin, made usually with phthalic anhydride, glycerol and fatty acids from vegetable oils.

*Alkyd wall paint—*A paint made from synthetic resins and oils. Usually dries flat; suitable for decorating and glazing.

Ammonia (NH_4OH)—Ammonia gas, dissolved in water; or, ordinary household ammonia, sold as Bo-Peep, Bright Sail, and many other trade names.

*Antiquing—*Broad term to describe a furniture-finishing technique that simulates what age and wear would have done. Includes one or more coats of flat enamel or other flat paint, and a coat of tinted glaze. After the enamel or paint base coats are applied, a transparent or opaque glaze is put on to give more depth of color.

Antiquing undercoat paint—A flat, oil-base, enamel-type paint, usually specifically labeled, "to be used as undercoating or base painting for glaze."

Artist's acrylic paint—See *acrylic paint*.

Base paint—See *antiquing undercoat paint*.

Cellulose wallpaper paste—See *synthetic resin wallpaper adhesive*.

Damar varnish—Varnish made from a natural resin obtained only in the East Indies; expensive and of very high quality.

Flat, oil-base wall paint—A kind of interior paint that dries to a dull, lusterless finish. Often called *alkyd*.

Flat paint—Any paint that dries with a dull, matte finish, without gloss or luster.

Garnet sandpaper—The abrasive used for this sandpaper is reddish and comes from the same source as the semiprecious gem *garnet*. More expensive than flint paper, but much longer-lasting, and cuts faster.

Glaze—A thinned varnish, tinted with different colors in oil, used as a finishing coat over antiquing base paint to soften, blend and mellow. Usually loaded with earth color pigments and less binder, with linseed oil base. Should dry flat.

Japan drier—A liquid drier containing varnish gum with a large proportion of metallic (lead, cobalt, manganese, etc.) salts added to hasten drying. Used in paints, varnishes, enamels.

Latex paint—Term used in connection with all resin and rubber emulsion paints. These materials thin with water, and the brushes used with them are washed in water. These paints have not proved suitable, in my experience, for decorating or glazing.

Lye (NaOH—sodium hydroxide)—A strong, impure alkali or caustic, sold under trade names such as Drano and others, for cleaning plumbing and drains. Also known as *Caustic soda*. Dangerous to use without proper skin and eye protection.

Magnesium carbonate—A mineral (also known as *magnesite*, $MgCO_3$) that is white and very light in weight. Used, for the purposes of this book, for rubbing on tracing paper to make a white carbon, enabling one to transfer designs to a dark surface.

Matte varnish—Acrylic polymer emulsion, made matte with hard wax and colloidal silica, sold as Liquitex Matte Varnish, used as a medium or thinner for painting with acrylic tube paints, and as a final protective coat over any acrylic painting.

Medium—The vehicle, usually a liquid, that pigment is suspended in to form paint; also, the liquid used to thin or extend the paint while it is applied.

Metal Treat—A preparation containing phosphoric acid, used to treat all metal surfaces, especially galvanized and aluminum, to insure good adhesion of primer. Prevents and removes rust.

Metallic wax—A wax incorporating gold, silver, copper, pewter, and other metallic powders. When rubbed on a surface, it leaves a thin coat of metallic finish. May be thinned with turpentine or mineral spirits and brushed on as a paint. Sold as Rub 'n Buff, Treasure Gold, and under other trade names.

Methanol—Another name for methyl alcohol. *See wood alcohol.*

Methyl alcohol—The chemical term for wood alcohol. *See wood alcohol.*

Mineral spirits—Petroleum product which has the same evaporation rate as turpentine; used to thin paint, clean brushes, and for any other purposes of a paint thinner.

Paraffin oil—A light-gravity mineral oil often used as a lubricant for sanding or rubbing a dried film of finishing material, such as varnish. In this book, used with rottenstone to rub down a final coat of varnish.

Patina—A film or coloring on a substance, generally believed to be ornamental, and indicative of age—such as glaze.

Penetrol—Paint additive that increases wetting action when added to any oil-base paint, making it flow more smoothly and adhere easily. Used on tight, granular rust in full strength to stop rust action, not to remove rust. May be added as rust preventative to any oil paint.

Plastic wood—A plastic preparation like soft putty, which when it is dry, looks like wood and can be varnished, painted, sawed, sanded, planed, drilled, or nailed. Used to patch and fill damaged furniture. Sold as Plastic Wood, Wood Dough, Wood Patch and under other trade names.

Polymer medium—Acrylic polymer emulsion, used to thin and extend acrylic paints in tubes. *See medium, also matte varnish.*

Primer—Paint applied next to the surface of material being painted. First coat in painting operation.

Rottenstone—A soft, siliceous (contains silica) limestone in finely pulverized form, used as an abrasive and polishing agent for dried varnish or other finishing materials. Also known as "tripoli."

Satin varnish—Varnish that dries to a finish with a luster similar to that of satin—between a full gloss and a semigloss luster; a dull luster. The new polyurethane and plastic varnishes fit this description; a satin finish is our goal.

Semigloss paint—Oil-base paint that dries to a sheen which is about halfway between dead flat finish and full gloss. Not suitable for decorating and antiquing, as this finish is too slick.

Shellac—Rosin extracted by parasitic insects from various trees in Southern Asia, dissolved in alcohol. Used, for the purposes of this book, as a sealer or primer for new or painted wood.

Spar varnish—A very durable, elastic, waterproof varnish, designed for severe service on exterior surfaces. Such a varnish must be resistant to rain, sunlight and heat. Originally used for coating masts and spars on sailing vessels.

Synthetic resin wallpaper adhesive—Wallpaper paste made from plastic or synthetic resin that dries clear and does not attract bugs. Cellulose wallpaper adhesive is also suitable.

Tack rag—Cloth impregnated with varnish used in wood finishing to remove abrasive dust from surface of wood, before applying finishing material.

Templet or *template*—A pattern, mold, or the like, usually consisting of a thin plate of wood or metal, serving as a gauge or guide in mechanical work.

Tinner's Red—A dark red primer for wood or metal. The rich color comes from red iron oxides, added as rust preventatives. Has excellent adherence and forms a tough, protective film over the surface. (Not *red lead*—that goes on bridges!)

Turpentine—Colorless, volatile liquid having a characteristic odor and taste. Obtained by distillation of the oleoresinous secretions found in living and dead pine trees.

White glue—That versatile, milky household glue made from polyvinyl acetate, sold under such brand names as Elmer's Glue-All or Sears Craftsman White Glue. A polyvinyl resin glue.

Wood alcohol—Poisonous alcohol obtained by destructive distillation of wood, also called *methyl alcohol* or *methanol*. The fumes of this alcohol can cause blindness, and if taken internally severe brain damage or death is the result.

INDEX